GETTING A FIX ON VOCABULARY

USING WORDS IN THE NEWS

to
Understand and Use
Prefixes, Suffixes,
Bases, and Compounds

Raymond C. Clark & Janie L. Duncan

PRO LINGUA ASSOCIATES

Published by Pro Lingua Associates

74 Cotton Mill Hill, Suite A315, Brattleboro, Vermont 05301
Orders: 800-366-4775
Phone: 802-257-7779
Email: Orders@ProLinguaAssociates.com
Webstore: www.ProLinguaAssociates.com
SAN : 216-0579

At Pro Lingua,
our objective is to foster
an approach to learning and teaching, which we
call Interplay, the interaction of language learners and teachers
with their materials, with the language and the culture,
and with each other in active, creative,
and productive play.

Acknowledgement for the use of copyrighted material is on page viii. All of the news stories in both articles and news broadcasts are completely fictitious.

ISBN 978-0-86647-270-8

This book was designed and set in Adobe Times by Arthur A. Burrows. Adobe Times, a digital font based on an early Twentieth Century type called Times New Roman, is at present one of the most popular type faces, and it is used by many newspapers. Being consistent in weight and color, with sharp neoclassical serifs, it is easy to read even when set small, photocopied, or printed badly. Newspaper headlines need to be strong and dramatic. Today many different faces are used, but faces designed by Giambattista Bodoni (1740-1813) are still popular. Bodoni, among the most prolific of type designers, lived in Parma, Italy, at the height of the Romantic era. His dark, geometric letters with a strong contrast between thick and thin lines make them stand out against more consistent and calligraphic faces like Times. The book was printed and bound by Royal Palm Press, Punta Gorda, Florida.

Printed in the United States of America.
Second edition, fifth printing, 2019
18,425 copies in print

Contents

Foreword
to the Teacher
Why use this book?

This text is designed for high-intermediate/advanced-level learners of English as a second language and high school-level English first-language speakers. An accompanying CD also offers optional listening practice that prefigures or echoes the reading passage that concludes each lesson.

The primary purpose of this book is to increase the learners' awareness of the morphology of English – bases, affixation, and compounding – and to help them develop their skill in word analysis. This awareness and skill can help turn unknown words into words that are, if not fully understood, at least partially meaningful, and by recognizing the part of speech of the affix (noun, verb, adjective, adverb), the learners can more easily grasp the meaning of whole sentences.

Secondly, an increased awareness of affixes and bases can facilitate vocabulary expansion by helping students see connections among various forms, e.g., contain, maintain, retain, unretained, detainable, detention. In this way, learning one word can lead to learning a bundle of words.

This text will also help develop spelling and pronunciation skills by identifying patterns that occur when bases and affixes are combined, e.g., *explode, explosion*.

A fourth purpose is to increase the learners' vocabulary. To this end, we have provided fictitious, "generic" news stories for reading practice at the end of each lesson. A similar version of the "newspaper" story is also available on CD as a "radio news broadcast." Although the primary purpose of these stories is to showcase selected bases, affixes, and compounds, the learners will also develop their knowledge of words and phrases that are commonly used in the media. The accompanying CD will also give the learners practice in following the discourse of typical radio and TV newscasts.

How to use the book

This book has been designed to facilitate self-directed learning. However, it would still be useful for the teacher to check that students are progressing satisfactorily, and to see if they have questions. Hence, a regular procedure, at its simplest, would be:

Assign the lesson for homework. The optional CD can also be assigned with the recommendation that the learner first listen to the CD to get an overview of the "news" content.

Follow up to see what questions the students have from the assignment.

Follow-up can also be more detailed:

Have the learners brainstorm words exhibiting morphemes that are the focus of the lesson (fill up the blackboard or poster paper).

Have the learners close their books while you read the news story aloud. Ask the them to tap their pencils on their desks every time you say a word that contains the featured morphemes. Alternatively, have them write it down.

Read the news story sentence by sentence (or paragraph by paragraph). After each sentence, ask a few questions: Who? What? When? Where? Why? How long? etc. Vary this approach by having learners read while you listen for pronunciation.

Give a quiz based on the featured morphemes or the news story.

Copy the news story and white out all the featured morphemes. Then re-copy the story and have the learners fill in the blanks.

Copy and bring in a real news story and have the learners go on a word hunt, circling the featured morphemes or all the morphemes that have been studied.

The text can also be used mostly as an in-class activity. In this situation, a typical pattern of work might be:

Introduce the featured affixes.

Go through the explanations, adding elaborations of your own.

Have the learners work individually or in pairs on the exercises, without looking at the answer key.

Go over the learners' answers, clarifying and explaining where necessary.

Read through the news story, or assign it for homework.

The optional CD can be used in a variety of ways.

1. You can initiate the lesson by playing the CD and writing some of the featured morphemes on the board. Then ask the learners to induce the form and meaning of the featured morpheme.

2. Play the CD just before assigning the "newspaper" reading. Or play it just after. The purpose is to hear the news and the morphemes in a different discourse context.

3. A list of the key words in each "newscast" begins on page 113, after the newscast scripts at the back of the book. You can have the students use this list in two ways.

   You can have them listen to the CD while looking at the key word list. Then have them read and/or read and listen to the script, highlighting the key words. When they are finished, they can go back to the list to check their work.

   Or you can play the CD while the students are looking at the script; have them highlight the featured words as they listen. To do this, the students need to focus on the morphemes used in the lesson (option 1) or to do the exercises before listening (option 2). Then have them check their work by looking at the key word list.

Acknowledgements

We would like to thank Mike Jerald for his "news" photographs on pages 4, 16, 50, 58, 70, and 74 and Pat Moran for his "courtroom sketch" of the Julio Doble trial on page 32. Thanks also to Cagle Cartoons for the cartoon "Exploders" on page 79 and the front cover. The cartoon was created by Petar Pismestrovic for Kleine Zeitung, Austria.

The use of other "news" photographs has been purchased from the archives of the Dreamstime.com Agency. The copyright to these photos is held by the photographers. The pictures of the staff of WPLA in order of appearance are Cindy Speakwell of The News at Noon, page 3 © Paul Prescott, Walter Conrad of The Evening News, page 9 © Lisa F. Young, Maria Ventura of The Morning Show, page 17 © Florian Ispas, and Jerry Michaels, WPLA Roving Reporter, page 91 © Carlos SantaMaria. The staff also appear on the back cover. On the title page, the photo of the newspaper is © Wieslaw File; the radio microphone is © Janet Hastings. News photos: Crash site on page 7 © Photooiasson, TransBoreal Bear on page 12 © Oliver Suckling, TV on page 16 © Marcus Gann EMJ, Prof. Brown-Archer on page 20 © Mtr, C. M. Unsap on page 22 © Wong Chee Yen, Candidates Contra and Changeless on page 25 © Marcin Balcerzak, R. J. Lee on page 36 © Imad Birkholz, Hamad III on page 40 © Christopher Hall Oran, Earthquake on page 46 © Ivan Hafizov, Global warming map on page 54 © 2014 Tim Osborn, Spies on page 62: Dr. Oui ©Tan Jace and Kitty Hawk © Nazira–g, NewlandiaStar on page 66 © Brent Reeves, Dr. Lalwani on page 78 © Nikhil Gangavane.

We would also like to thank the many students at the Center for International Banking Studies in Istanbul, who used the preliminary edition of this book. Their comments and questions were very helpful, as were the suggestions of our colleague Melinda Taplin.

Raymond C. Clark and Janie L. Duncan
June 1989, August 2008

Introduction

There are thousands of words in English. Learning these words is a big problem for learners of English. However, there are ways to solve this problem. One way is to become familiar with the process of word formation in English. Take for example, the phrase:

Underground Explosions

The word *underground* is really two separate words, *under* and *ground*. This illustrates a process of word formation that is called **compounding**. Many English words are formed this way.

The word *explosions* is formed by a process called **affixation**. A **base** carries the main meaning of the word, and **affixes** add to the meaning. The base here is ***plod,*** which comes from Latin and means "making a noise by clapping the hands together," or "noise."

In the word *explosions* there are three different affixes. ***Ex-*** is attached in front of the base and is called a **prefix**. ***-sion*** is attached after the base and is called a **suffix**. Another suffix, ***-s***, indicates the word is plural, and it is attached to the singular form of the word *explosion*.

Therefore, an analysis of the word shows us this:

ex-	***plo(d)***	***-sion***	***-s***
out of, from	noisy	the act of (also shows the word is a noun)	plural

As you can see from the example, the process of analyzing a word into its parts will not always give an exact meaning for the word. Words often change their meanings with the passage of time, especially after they are borrowed from one language and put to use in another language. But analysis will help. It is especially important and useful to learn the affixes because there are not many of them and they are used a lot in English. A chart of the affixes that we will study in this book appears on page 2.

You can also see that it is helpful, if not necessary, to know the meaning of the base in order to fully understand the word. But the list of bases is very long and we would not expect you to learn or know them all. In this book we will work only with some of the more common bases. There is a glossary of common bases in the back of this book.

You will also see in the example that there are some spelling and pronunciation changes when affixes are added to bases.

Word analysis is not an exact, precise process which will always give you the complete meaning. But developing some skill in taking words apart will help you better understand what you read, and it will help you increase your vocabulary.

Throughout the text, we have used readings and vocabulary that you will frequently see in the news. The news stories are not real, but they are similar to news stories that appear regularly in newspapers. So this book will also introduce you to words that you will see again and again in any English-language newspaper. When you have finished this book, you can continue your vocabulary development with the help of the daily newspaper.

In the back of this book there is an answer key so you can check your answers to the exercises.

Affix Chart

Lesson Number	Prefixes		Function/Meaning	Lesson Number	Suffixes		Function/Meaning
6	un- in-	non-	Negative	4	-er		"Doer" Noun
7	anti- a- dis-	mal- mis-		5	-ist -ian	-ant -ary	
				9	-en -ify	-ate -ize	Verb
8	uni- mono- bi- tri- pan-	multi- semi- poly- equi-	Quantity	10	-ance -ity -hood	-ship -ness	Noun
9	en-	be-	Verb	11	-ion -ment -ism	-age -dom	
16	pre- post- inter-	intra- extra-	Position	12	-able -less	-al -en	Adjective
17	super- sur- epi- hyper-	sub- hypo- para-	Relationship	13	-ful -y	-ous -ary	
				14	-ish -ic	-ive	
18	ex- in- ad-	ab- trans- pro-	Movement	15	-ly -ward	-wise	Adverb
19	de- re-	se-					
20	syn- co-	contra- ob-	With or Against				

Lesson 1

Inflections

In the word *explosion* we saw that the final affix *-s* made the word plural. This kind of affix is called an **inflection**, and it is somewhat different from *ex-* and *-sion*. It is really a grammatical suffix, and almost every noun in English can be made plural by simply adding *-s*. We say "almost" because there are irregular noun plurals such as **man/men.** Also, there are some spelling changes in English when inflections are affixed, so that the plural of *dish* is *dishes*, and the plural of *dictionary* is *dictionaries.* Also note that irregular verbs can be considered inflected, and that some verb inflections function like adjectives. For example, *suspected* can be an adjective.

The eight inflectional suffixes in English are:

Inflectional Suffix	Example	Grammatical Function
-ed	exploded	past tense or past participle
-en	hidden	past participle
-ing	planning	progressive form or present participle
-s	continues	third person singular verb
-s	explosions	plural
-'s	prosecutor's	possessive marker
-er	larger	comparative
-est	largest	superlative

Exercises

A. Read the following article once. Do it rapidly for general comprehension. Then go through the story again, and highlight the inflectional suffixes. Check your answers with the answer key.

B. Look in the glossary of bases at the back of the book for the meaning of in***vestig***ation, su***spect,*** and de***tain.*** Whenever you see new words, look for their bases and check their meanings in the glossary.

Terrorist Conspiracy Uncovered

STATESBORO (PLN) A spokesperson said today that federal police have detained five suspected terrorists. The police also discovered explosives hidden in a Westside warehouse, and several automatic weapons were taken from the apartment of one of the suspected terrorists.

The police raided four separate locations Thursday and apparently prevented a terrorist attack, a spokesperson for the prosecutor's office said in a telephone interview.

The detainees were under investigation for criminal conspiracy. Homeland Security sources claim they have been planning an attack to be carried out in an unnamed neighboring country.

Intelligence officers discovered the conspiracy, and warrants have been issued for the arrest of three ringleaders, the intelligence agency said.

Federal undercover agents, who normally head antiterrorism investigations, were handling the case.

Although this was not the agency's largest roundup of suspected terrorists, it is expected that the list of arrests may grow longer as the investigation continues.

TERRORIST HIDEOUT on West 164th St. raided by Feds Thursday.   MJ PHOTO

Lesson 2

Cindy Speakwell • WPLA Newsbreak

CD track 2   Radio script page 92

TODAY'S RADIO NEWS

Airliner, Military Aircraft Collide

Compounds

Underground is a compound word. It is two words that are joined together to form a new word. Each part of the compound has a meaning. Usually it is fairly easy to understand the meaning of the compound word. But sometimes it helps to look at the context in which the word appears. This means you should look at the words that precede and follow the word you are analyzing.

Exercises

A. The word ***underground*** is fairly easy to understand. It is ***under*** and ***ground***, meaning beneath the surface of the earth. Can you guess the meaning of these?

> spokesperson
> ringleader
> undercover
> roundup
> warehouse

If you have any difficulty, go back to the reading in Lesson 1 and look at the context. Then guess the meaning. Finally, check your guesses with the help of a dictionary.

1. spokesperson   Guess _____

                   Dictionary _____

2. ringleader   Guess _____

                   Dictionary _____

3. undercover   Guess _____

                   Dictionary _____

4. roundup   Guess _____

                   Dictionary _____

5. warehouse   Guess _____

                   Dictionary _____

Looking at the context is a useful thing to do. If you cannot easily analyze a new word, be sure to study the context.

Answers for Lesson 2 on page 81   **Lesson 2: Compounds** • 5

B. Sometimes compound words are hyphenated. This means there is a line, called a hyphen, between the two parts of the word. Here are some examples. Give the meaning of the hyphenated compound. Try to do this by studying the context of the compound.

1. According to the Medical Association, the new technique could lower risks for heart-attack victims.

    heart-attack _____

2. The attack is likely to increase support for the conservative right-wing political party.

    right-wing _____

3. The head of the seven-member committee has resigned.

    seven-member _____

4. The negotiator has arranged for a cease-fire between the warring countries.

    cease-fire _____

5. Investigators have concluded a five-year investigation of terrorism.

    five-year _____

6. The two nations have agreed to hold high-level talks.

    high-level _____

7. A government-backed militia has counterattacked.

    government-backed _____

8. At the new airport all of the waiting areas are smoke-free, and there is now a duty-free shop where you do not pay tax on purchases.

    smoke-free _____

    duty-free _____

9. The Boeing 737 is a twin-engine aircraft.

    twin-engine _____

C. You may notice, as you read the news, that numbers are often used as part of a compound phrase, for example, a *three-day visit.* On the lines below write some compound phrases, similar to the example. Be careful that you don't make the second word of the hyphenated compound plural. For example, a *three-day visit* not a *three-days visit.*

_____ _____ _____ _____

_____ _____ _____ _____

D. Noun compounds are normally pronounced with the heaviest stress on the first part of the word. Practice saying these common compounds with stress on the first part of the word.

airline	thunderstorm	rainstorm
turbojet	daybreak	lifejackets
takeoff	airport	mainland
jetliner	seaside	frogmen

E The following story contains several compound words. First read the story for general comprehension; then read it for details; and finally highlight all the compounds.

Airliner, Military Aircraft Collide

GULFSIDE (PLN) The national radio, NRT, announced today that an outbound turbojet aircraft operated by the state-owned airline NATIONAIR collided with a military fighter-bomber. The collision occurred shortly after Flight 43's takeoff from Gulfside Airport. Flight 43 is a regularly scheduled hour-long flight to Pelagia.

There were no eyewitnesses to the midair collision. It was first believed that the twin-engine jetliner had been struck by lightning. A heavy thunderstorm hit the area shortly before daybreak.

It is assumed that both aircraft went down in the Pacific Gulf. An airline spokeswoman has confirmed that the airliner was enroute to the popular seaside resort of Pelagia.

Air-sea rescue teams dispatched to the area began the search for survivors in a heavy rainstorm. So far, none have been seen in the shark-infested waters, although several life jackets were seen floating fifteen air-miles from the mainland coast. Navy frogmen will begin an underwater search for the wreckage when weather conditions permit.

CRASH SITE in shark-infested waters.   *Daily Newsphoto Inc.*

Lesson 3

Some Common Bases

Most of the work in this book focuses on affixes, which are attached to bases, also called roots. Sometimes the base is a word, like *fix*. Sometimes the base is not a word itself, like ***plod***, as in *explode*.

Many bases that are not words by themselves come from Latin. The list of Latin bases that are used in English is very long, and it is not possible to memorize the list. It would be like trying to memorize a small dictionary. However, there are some Latin bases that occur frequently in English. In this lesson we will look at some of the most common bases.

The base forms that are used in the exercise are:

Motion	Action	Miscellaneous
duct	clud	cred
grad	ceive	tens
ceed	ject	claim
port	tract	rect
mot	tain	dict
mit	rupt	med
	cid	scrib
	act	pos
		struct

Exercises

A1. The bases in this exercise all suggest some kind of motion. Match the motion words below with the underlined bases in the sentences.

Motion Words

a. carry	c. send	e. move along
b. move	d. go in steps	f. lead

Sentences

1. He con<u>duct</u>ed the Thyme Orchestra.
2. <u>Gradu</u>ally the fighting subsided.
3. Let's pro<u>ceed</u> carefully. This is an important decision.
4. Let's bring a <u>port</u>able radio with us.
5. He didn't lose his job, but he was de<u>mot</u>ed, and his salary was reduced.
6. This radio can trans<u>mit</u> a signal for 100 kilometers.

A2. Can you guess at the meaning of the underlined word?

1. Copper is a good <u>conductor</u> of electricity

   _____

2. He <u>graduated</u> from State University.

   _____

3. After the heavy rain, the water slowly <u>receded</u>, and the river did not flood the town.

   _____

4. Iran <u>exports</u> oil.

   _____

5. She was <u>promoted</u> to vice-president.

   _____

6. The <u>mission</u> to the moon was completed successfully.

   _____

B1. The bases in this exercise all have a general meaning of action. Match these action words with the underlined base in the sentences.

Action Words

a. get, take	d. throw	g. pull
b. happen	e. break	h. act
c. close, shut	f. hold, keep	

Sentences

1. The instructions were not <u>clud</u>ed in the package.
2. He never re<u>ceiv</u>ed my proposal.
3. The astronauts' safety capsule was e<u>ject</u>ed from their spacecraft.
4. The dentist ex<u>tract</u>ed all his wisdom teeth.
5. The detainee <u>tri</u>ed to escape
6. The strike has dis<u>rupt</u>ed air travel throughout the East.
7. We met by coin<u>cid</u>ence; it wasn't planned.
8. The crowd re<u>act</u>ed violently when the police arrived.

B2. Can you guess the meaning of the underlined words?

1. The <u>conclusion</u> of the story was quite surprising.

   _____

2. Did you get a <u>receipt</u> for the purchase?

   _____

3. Their proposal was <u>rejected</u> and so they won't get the contract.

   _____

4. Did you <u>subtract</u> your expenses? It looks like you forgot them.

   _____

5. Please <u>retain</u> this copy of your bill for your records.

   _____

6. There was an <u>accident</u> at the corner of Main and State Streets.

   _____

7. She is an important <u>activist</u> in the Save the Whales campaign.

   _____

C1. These bases have a variety of meanings. Match the words below with the underlined base in the sentences.

Words

a. talk, shout	d. rule, manage	g. stretch, tighten
b. write	e. believe, trust	h. place, put
c. say	f. carry	i. build, develop

1. _____ The bank is going to give him <u>cred</u>it.
2. _____ After three days of in<u>tens</u>ive talks the two sides agreed.
3. _____ "No!" he ex<u>claim</u>ed.
4. _____ The di<u>rect</u>or will see you in his office.
5. _____ Some people try to pre<u>dict</u> the future.
6. _____ They are re<u>duc</u>ing the number of missiles.
7. _____ Can you pre<u>scribe</u> some medicine for me?
8. _____ The king was de<u>pos</u>ed by the army and sent away.
9. _____ The earthquake caused a lot of <u>struct</u>ural damage.

C2. Can you guess the meaning of the underlined words?

1. It was an <u>incred</u>ible story.

   _____

2. "Relax!" she said. "You're too <u>tens</u>e."

   _____

3. He <u>claim</u>ed that he had never been at the scene of the crime.

   _____

4. There are many <u>regul</u>ations concerning the use of guns.

   _____

5. The <u>dict</u>ator was forced to run for his life.

   _____

6. The <u>medi</u>ator got the two sides to agree.

   _____

7. The <u>inscript</u>ion on the stone was very old and hard to read.

   _____

8. That beautiful model has <u>pos</u>ed for many pictures.

   _____

9. The <u>instruct</u>ions on the new machine were not very clear.

   _____

D. Read the following article once for general comprehension. Then read it for details and highlight words with the bases we have studied in this lesson.

Nature Society Successful: Wilderness Saved

PORT NORD, Borealis. (PP) – Today the Nature Society claimed a major victory in its fight to save the Boreal Wilderness. The society has been conducting a "Save Boreas" campaign for the past five years, and at a national media conference, Society President Forrest Woods announced that the National Congress is going to take an incredibly important action by refusing to allow oil exploration in the wilderness.

Five years ago, the government predicted that the world's shrinking supply of oil would require drilling in the Boreal Wilderness. The United Federal Party, under the leadership of Senator Les Dewit, reacted by proposing to open the Wilderness to oil exploration. The Nature Society objected to the government's plan, claiming that even oil exploration would disrupt the delicate ecological balance of the wilderness. Drilling, extracting, and transporting oil would all be disruptive, and oil spills, especially as oil was transported to Port Nord, could be exceedingly damaging. Motor traffic alone would inject air and noise pollution into the serene boreal forest, exposing the plant and animal life to unnecessary tension and stress.

The endanged TransBoreal Bear   NatureNews Photo

The Society's own intensive study of the area concluded that constructing oil fields in the Wilderness would result in habitat destruction that could never be corrected. The incredible beauty of the area would be lost forever. The study pointed out that the Boreal forest zone contained many unique life forms. Many Boreal plant and animal species, including the TransBoreal Bear, would become extinct.

Woods went on to say that any activity, even preliminary and limited exploration, would have an impact. The region would gradually lose wildlife habitat, and the last remaining herd of Boreal Elk would be endangered.

President Woods described the saving of the wilderness as a great success.

Lesson 4

The *-er* Noun Suffix

One of the most common suffixes in English is *-er,* also spelled *-or* and *-ar.* It usually means "a person who (does something)."

teacher – a person who teaches

banker – a person who works in a bank

driver – a person who drives (a car)

player – a person who plays (a game)

collector – a person who collects (something)

beggar – a person who begs

It is not always easy to know which spelling to use, and there are other spelling problems, too. Look at *driver*, for example. The base is *drive*. When *er* is added, one of the *e's* is dropped. And with *beg*, the final consonant is doubled: *beggar.*

• *Note:* Be careful that you don't confuse this *-er* suffix with the *-er* suffix that indicates comparison: *big > bigger*   *His car is **bigger** than mine.*

A few *-er* words do not refer to people. They refer to a machine or thing that does something.

computer – a machine that computes

tractor – a vehicle that pulls things

There is an *-ee* suffix which shows that the person is the receiver of the action, not the doer of the action. In many cases there is a corresponding *-er* suffix.

employer – the owner of a business who employs workers

employee – the workers who are employed by the owner of the business

And there are a very few *-er* suffixes that are spelled *-eer.*

mountaineer – one who climbs mountains

Answers for Lesson 4 on page 81

Exercises

A. Rewrite these common words with an **-er/-or/-ar** suffix. There will be some spelling changes so check your spelling with the answers in the back of the book.

report	_____	march	_____
credit	_____	kidnap	_____
write	_____	direct	_____
profess	_____	design	_____
buy	_____	trade	_____
lead	_____	vote	_____
manage	_____	riot	_____
employ	_____	law	_____
prosecute	_____	foreign	_____
work	_____	survive	_____
fly	_____	deal	_____
prison	_____	photograph	_____
plan	_____	demonstrate	_____
command	_____	advise	_____
inspect	_____	support	_____
export	_____	govern	_____
farm	_____	murder*	_____
hijack	_____	forecast	_____
lie	_____	act	_____
travel	_____	interpret	_____
investigate	_____	office	_____
negotiate	_____	defect	_____

*** Note:** A few English words end with **-er/or/ar,** but these endings are not suffixes. They are part of the word. For example: *labor, murder, number, border, corner.* Add some below.

_____ _____ _____ _____

B. A few *-er/or* words are attached to bases that are not words.
Use the list below to fill in the blanks.

soldier	minister	traitor
member	doctor	passenger
ambassador	chancellor	mayor
neighbor	victor	

1. A person who travels in a car or plane is a _____ .

2. A person who cares for sick people is a _____ .

3. A person who belongs to an organization is a _____ .

4.   A person who is in the army is a _____ .

5. A person who is in charge of an embassy is an _____ .

6. A person who is the political leader of a city is a _____ .

7. A person who defects to another country can be called a _____ .

8. The leader of some countries is called a _____ .

9. The person who is in charge of a ministry is a _____ .

10. A person who lives near you is a _____ .

11. A person who wins and gets the victory is a _____ .

C. In some cases the suffix *-er* indicates "a machine or thing that. . ."
Match these *er* things with their correct definitions.

__ bomber   a. a ship that carries airplanes

__ fighter   b. a device that cooks food

__ jetliner   c. a plane that attacks other planes

__ tanker   d. an electronic device that does computation

__ computer   e. an aircraft that does not have wings

__ aircraft carrier   f. a device that sends radio or TV signals

__ printer   g. a plane that carries passengers

__ transmitter   h. a ship that carries oil

__ recorder   i. a plane that attacks targets on the ground

__ helicopter   j. an instrument that records sound

__ cooker*   k. a machine that prints

* *Note*: a person who cooks is a *cook*.

D. The **-ee** suffix shows us the person is the receiver of a corresponding **-er** suffix. Complete these sentences:

1. The _____ is employed by the _____ .

2. The _____ was detained by the police.

3. The _____ trains the _____ .

4. The _____ pays the _____ .

5. The letter is addressed to the _____ .

E. Another variation of the **-er** suffix is the **-eer** suffix. There are not many of this type. Here are some:

1. A person who makes a profit is a _____ .

2. A person who writes pamphlets is a _____ .

3. A person who is involved in an illegal racket is a _____ .

4. A person who sells things at an auction is an _____ .

5. A person who works voluntarily, that is without pay, is a _____ .

6. A person who works with engines is an _____ .

F. Read the following article once for general comprehension. Then read it for details, and highlight the words with **-er/-or/-ar** suffixes.

Negotiator Meets With Kidnappers

Antarctican Ambassador

ATLANTIA (PLN) — A government negotiator who has been meeting with kidnappers of the Antarctican ambassador to Atlantis met with reporters yesterday and released a statement from the Ambassador's captors. The kidnappers, identified as members of the little-known AMSAT faction, have demanded the release of all political prisoners in exchange for the ambassador. The ambassador was abducted two weeks ago, along with his political adviser and interpreter. The leader of the AMSAT group has also issued a warning to all foreigners now in Atlantis that unless AMSAT's demands are met, foreign workers and travelers will be in danger. Meanwhile, in downtown Atlantia, the mayor and his councilors met with demonstrators who marched on City Hall. The marchers, reportedly supporters of AMSAT, have urged that the military prison commander be dismissed on grounds that political detainees have been tortured. The mayor assured the marchers that a special investigator would be appointed to look into the matter.

Lesson 5

Other "Doer" Suffixes: *-ist, -ian, -ant/-ent* and "Place" Suffixes: *-ary/-ery/-ory/-ry*

In addition to **-er** and its variants, there are three other suffixes that also mean "doer" of the activity: **-ist, -ian,** and **-ant**. There are some pronunciation or spelling changes when these suffixes are attached to a base.

> **type** – typist
> **diet** – dietician
> **study** – student

Notice that the **-ian** suffix is often spelled **-cian**. For example, a hairdresser who also helps women with their hands and faces to make them beautiful is called a **beautician**; someone who does magic is a **magician**. Also, many nationality names use this suffix or **-an**: *Canadian, Italian, Ethiopian, Mexican, Tibetan, Moroccan.*

- *Note:* Not all words ending in **-ant/-ent** are "doer" words. *Vacant* and *permanent* are adjectives.

-ary, -ery, -ory, and **-ry** are suffixes that often mean "a place where ..." For example, a **winery** is a place where wine is made and a **granary** is a place where grain is stored.

However, there are many irregularities with this suffix, and the exact meaning of the word may not refer to a place. For example, it may refer to a person who does something, a type of material, or the study or practice of some subject.

Secretary is a person, not a place for secrets. *Stationery* means writing paper. *Forestry* is the management of forests. *Chemistry* is the study of chemicals.

- *Note:* **-ary** may also be an adjective suffix. It means "engaged in or connected with." We will study this suffix in lesson 13. For example: *temporary, primary, stationary.*

Answers for Lesson 5 on page 82

Exercises

A. In the following sentences, write the appropriate *-ist* word.

1. A person who is involved in science is a _____ .

2. People who work in the fields of sociology, psychology, and psychiatry are

   _____ , _____ , and _____ .

3. A person who is involved in economics is an _____ .
   a. Capitalism is practiced by _____ .
   b. Socialism is practiced by _____ .
   c. Communism is practiced by _____ .

4. Some writers:
   a. A person who writes dramas is a _____ .
   b. A person who writes novels is a _____ .
   c. A person who writes columns in a newspaper is a _____ (also called a journalist).

5. Some musicians:
   a. A _____ plays the guitar.   d. A _____ plays cello.
   b. A _____ plays the violin.   e. A _____ plays the flute.
   c. A _____ plays the piano.

6. Politicians who are realistic are _____ , and if they are idealistic, they are _____ .

7. A person who is very active, especially in political matters, is an _____ . And if the person wants to have no government (anarchy), they are an _____ . An activist in environmental matters is an _____ . Ecology is the science of environmental balance. A person who studies it is an _____ .

8. Three criminals:
   One who burns buildings (the crime of arson): _____ .
   One who practices terror: _____ .
   One who rapes: _____ .

9. A person who tours a foreign country is a _____ .
   A person who drives a motor car is a _____ .

B. Match these *-ian* words with the appropriate description.

1. __ politician   a. Albert Einstein
2. __ musician   b. One who works in government
3. __ mathematician (and physicist)   c. a doctor
4. __ technician   d. the opposite of military
5. __ physician   e. a guitarist
6. __ civilian   f. one who operates technical instruments

C. Complete the following with an *-ant/-ent* word. Use the list of bases below.

   occup-   pati-   dissid-   immigr-   resid-
   account-   migr-   consult-   oppon-

1. a worker who migrates from place to place: a _____ worker.
2. a person who opposes another: an _____ .
3. a person who charges money for giving advice: a _____ .
4. a person who gives financial advice: an _____ .
5. a person who occupies a place: an _____ .
6. a person who is sick: a _____ .
7. a person who immigrates into a country: an _____ .
8. a person who disagrees with the government: a _____ .
9. a person who lives in a place: a _____ .

D. Fill in the blanks with one of these "place where" words.

   library   territory   bakery   directory
   laboratory   factory   mortuary   diary
   treasury   armory   chemistry   dictionary

1. Another word for "weapons" is "arms." Weapons would be kept in an _____ .
2. Bread is baked in a _____ .
3. Words are found in a _____ .
4. Telephone numbers are found in a _____ .
5. Daily notes are kept in a _____ .
6. A scientist works in a _____ .
7. Books are kept in a _____ .
8. The _____ department is concerned with money.
9. Goods are produced in a _____ .
10. Siberia is a huge _____ in Northern Russia.
11. Dead people are kept in a _____ before they are buried.
12. The study of matter is _____ .

E. Many nationalities are spelled with an *-ian* or *-an* suffix. Can you name a few?

   _____   _____   _____

   _____   _____   _____

Lesson 5: Other "Doer" Suffixes and "Place" Suffixes: *-ist, -ian, -ant, -ary* • **19**

F. Read the following selection first for general comprehension, then for details. Highlight all the words with suffixes that mean "one who" or "place where."

Awards for Artists and Scientists

Prof. Brown-Archer, geneticist

NORBERG, Nordlandia (PLN) The Academy of Arts and Sciences today announced this year's winners in the fields of science, literature, ecology, music, and economics. The winners will each receive a cash prize of $50,000, according to awards panelist Dr. Arthur Andrews.

Physicist Nils Groenig, notified of his award while working in his laboratory, celebrated with his research assistants by toasting them with a bottle of champagne. Botanist Anna Brown-Archer, a professor at the University of Jackson, received the award for her work in plant genetics. The third scientist cited by the Academy was Dr. Rolf Steinmetz, a chemist at the University of Overberg.

The novelist and dramatist Pedro Garcia, an Antillian, was named the recipient of the literature prize. His latest novel, *The Diary of an Idealist,* was acclaimed by the awards committee as a major contribution to world literature. The author, an outspoken dissident, is now a resident of Mexteca.

In the field of music, the award went to composer and pianist Gregor Kosnowski. Long considered one of the world's outstanding musicians, Kosnowski is best known for his piano concertos. A proponent of neo-romanticism, he is the resident conductor of the Thyme Conservatory of Music.

This year marked the first year that a prize was given to an environmentalist. Robert Rackham, a well-known forestry consultant and environmental activist, was praised for his work on the effects of deforestation in tropical rain forests.

The prize for economics was won by Martin Greenberg, whose recent book, *The Proletarian and the Capitalist,* is rapidly becoming a classic in its field.

Lesson 6

Negative Prefixes: *un-, in-, non-*

The word "prefix" has the prefix **pre-**, which means "before." Prefixes come at the beginning of a word. In this lesson and the one that follows, we will look at a group of prefixes that have a negative meaning.

One of the most common negative prefixes is **un-**, which means "not."

unimportant – not important

Similar to **un-** is **in-**. This prefix, however, has different spellings.
Sometimes it is spelled **im-, il-,** or **ir-**.

> **in + active** = inactive
> **in + perfect** = imperfect (**in-** becomes **im-** before *b, m,* and *p*)
> **in + legal** = illegal (**in-** becomes **il** before *l*)
> **in + regular** = irregular (**in-** becomes **ir-** before *r*)

> • *Note:* There is a prefix **in-** which means "in" or "into," as in **inhabitant** or **immigrant**.

Another common negative prefix is **non-**, which also means "not."

nonresident – not a resident

If the base begins with a capital letter, the prefix **non-** is usually attached to the base with a hyphen.

non-European

Exercises

A. You already know many words that begin with the prefix **un-**. List some below and compare them with a friend or a teacher, or check them in the dictionary.

_____   _____   _____
_____   _____   _____
_____   _____   _____
_____   _____   _____
_____   _____   _____

B. In the list below, add the prefix **in-** and its variants **im-, ir-, il-** to the base form.

___dependent	___perfect	___balance	___sane
___mature	___moral	___secure	___literate
___responsible	___capable	___logical	___proper
___definite	___direct	___rational	

C. Complete these sentences with a word that is prefixed with *non-*.

1. She doesn't smoke. She's a _____.
2. They are not Moslems. They are _____.
3. He does not write fiction. He writes only _____.
4. This flight does not stop between New York and London. It is _____.
5. Gandhi was against violence. He practiced _____.
6. This doesn't make sense. It's _____.
7. These chemicals are not toxic. They are _____.
8. He never conformed. He was a _____.
9. He didn't pay his debts. He was guilty of _____.
10. This population is not an Arab population. It is _____.
11. You aren't a member of the club. You're a _____.
12. The World Bank has a lot of loans that are not performing. They are _____ loans.

D. In the following story there are several negative prefixes, and a few **in-** prefixes that mean "in" or "into." Highlight the words with negative prefixes.

Nonresident Policy Questioned

LIP Leader C. M. Unsap

KAPITALIA, Lowland (PLN) – The leader of the Lowland Independent Party (LIP), C. M. Unsap, yesterday called for the government to take action on the "nonresident" problem.

Citing statistics released by the Lowland Immigration Department, the opposition leader pointed out that in the past five years over 7,000 Highlanders have been granted refugee status in Lowland, and an estimated 20,000 others have entered the country illegally.

So far, the Lowland government has been uninterested in stopping the flow because illegal entrants have been willing to take jobs that most Lowlanders find unattractive and financially unrewarding, according to Unsap.

Mr. Unsap also pointed out that the Department of Labor has released statistics showing that unemployment among Lowlanders has been steadily increasing. Unskilled Lowland workers have been especially hard hit, leading to a growing anti-Highlander sentiment that erupted in riots last spring in Kapitalia.

Also taking aim at the government's policy toward refugees, Unsap claimed that few, if any, of the refugees were leaving Highland for political reasons, and that unemployment in Highland is the real reason for the influx of so-called refugees, most of whom are uneducated and illiterate.

Calling the government's attitude toward the problem irresponsible, Unsap also warned that an unlimited influx of non-Lowlanders would be a serious strain on the country's already inadequate social services, leading to further unrest among Lowland's unemployed.

Lesson 7

Negative Prefixes: *anti-, a-, dis-, mal-, mis-*

In Lesson 6 we looked at negative prefixes that generally mean "not." In this lesson we will study some additional prefixes that have negative meanings.

anti- means against, opposite, or opposing.

> **antinuclear** – opposing nuclear (energy or warfare)

> • *Note:* there is also a prefix *ante-* that means "before" or "earlier," but there are not many words with this prefix.

a- means "not" or "without." It is also spelled *an-* when it is prefixed to a word that begins with a vowel.

> **a + political** = apolitical – not political
>
> **a + archy** = anarchy – without rule or government

dis- means "not," "apart from," "separate." It is also spelled *dif-* when prefixed to a word that begins with *f*, and in some cases, it is spelled *di-*. (And be careful that you don't confuse this with another prefix *di-*, which means "two.")

> **dis + agree** = disagree – to not agree
>
> **dis + connect** = disconnect – to separate a connnecton
>
> **dis + fuse** = diffuse – to spread
>
> **dis + verge** = diverge – to go in different directions

mal- means "bad," "badly," or "poor."

> **malnutrition** – bad or poor nutrition

mis- also means "bad," but it can also mean "wrong" or "fail."

> **misfortune** – bad fortune
>
> **miscalculate** – to calculate wrongly
>
> **misfire** – to fail to fire properly; "Her gun misfired."

contra- is a prefix with a negative sense, meaning "opposed" or "against." It will also be seen in Lessons 16 and 20.

Exercises

A. Give a short definition of the *anti-* words in the following sentences.

1. The plane was shot down by antiaircraft guns.

   _____

2. The Pro-Life group is in favor of antiabortion legislation.

   _____

3. The two enemies could not hide their mutual antipathy.

   _____

4. The Jewish delegation accused them of anti-Semitism.

   _____

5. This new antitrust law is designed to encourage more competition.

   _____

6. Synonyms are two words that have the same meaning.
   What are antonyms? (Notice the irregular spelling.)

   _____

B. Add the prefix *a-* or *an-* to the following list of bases. Check the unfamiliar words in your dictionary.

   _____typical   _____esthetic   _____theism

   _____archy   _____sexual   _____pathy

   _____political   _____nonymous   _____aerobic

   _____moral   _____morphous   _____symmetry

C. *dis-* can be prefixed to many words. Make a list of some that you know and compare your list with a friend, a teacher, or the dictionary.

   _____

   _____

   _____

D. Below is a list of *mis-* and *mal-* words without their prefixes. See if you can match them with the proper prefix. You may make a few mismatches, but that's OK. Everybody makes mistakes.

   _____behave   _____content   _____practice

   _____judge   _____manage   _____fit

   _____fortune   _____function   _____lead

   _____nutrition   _____guide   _____adjusted

   _____print   _____place   _____spell

E. Highlight the words with negative prefixes *dis-, mis-, mal-, a-, anti-*.

Candidates Disagree
Changeless Claims Lead in Polls

Changeless vs. Contra   *PLN PHOTO*

CAPITALIAS, D.N. (PLN) In a nationally televised debate last night, the two leading candidates for president carried out a lively exchange that sharply differentiated their views on diverse issues.

I. M. Contra, speaking first, challenged the incumbent administration's record on environmental matters, claiming that the Conservative Union Party was "at best apathetic in its support of antipollution measures." Contra also attacked the administration's economic policies, claiming that mismanagement of the economy was bringing the nation close to "financial ruin and a state of unregulated anarchy."

In response, Dr. Changeless lashed out at Contra, calling her and her followers a "bunch of malcontents and misfits who would lead the country down the dusty road of disruption and disturbance." Dr. Changeless labeled Contra's Everyman Party the "AEP or Anti-Everything Party," and charged that its leadership was "riddled with misguided and maladjusted atheists."

Contra responded to Changeless' attacks with sharp criticism of the administration's handling of the Robb scandal, claiming that it was common knowledge that Robb had misappropriated funds and that the whole affair was a "malignant growth on the nation." She further claimed that the President had been misled and misinformed by her advisers. In Contra's words, "Robb should have been dismissed immediately." Contra closed her remarks with a final attack, saying that if Dr. Changeless were a medical doctor she would be guilty of malpractice and her patient, the republic, would soon be dead of governmental malnutrition.

In her closing statement, Dr. Changeless defended her administration and pointed to the divisive nature of the Everyman Party's campaign as an indication of the amoral nature of the opposition party.

Claiming a 10-point lead in the latest polls, Dr. Changeless insisted that the voters would once again reject the opposition as unworthy to lead the country. "Remember the misgovernment of the 60s," she warned, "and don't make that mistake again. Your faith in my leadership is not misplaced." She concluded by saying that the opposition's tactics had misfired and that her Conservative Union Party would be victorious again.

Lesson 8

Maria Ventura • WPLA THE MORNING SHOW
Pan-Equatorians Meet

CD track 8   Radio script page 98

TODAY'S
RADIO NEWS

Quantity Prefixes: *uni-, mono-, bi-, tri-, pan-, multi-, semi-, poly-, equi-*

As you might guess, quantity prefixes indicate numbers, portions, or amounts of the bases to which they are affixed. You will encounter many of these prefixes in technical, scientific, and economic words that deal with measurements, comparisons, or descriptions of size or number. They do occur in everyday speech, however, and knowing their meanings can multiply your vocabulary.

Prefixes	Meanings
uni-	one
mono-/ mon-	one, single, or alone
bi-/ bin-	two, at intervals of two, or twice during ...
tri-	three, occurring at intervals of three, occurring three times during ...
pan-	all
multi-	many, much
semi-	half, partial, occurring twice
poly-	more than one, much, many
equi-	equal, equally

Answers for Lesson 8 on page 83

Exercises

A. Use the meanings from the list on the previous page to help you define the words below:

Definitions

1. bicycle   a vehicle mounted on _____ wheels
2. tricycle   a vehicle mounted on _____ wheels
3. unicycle   a vehicle mounted on _____ wheel
4. monolingual   a person who knows _____ language
5. bilingual   a person who knows _____ languages
6. equidistant   a place that is the _____ distance from two other places
7. _____   having or speaking three languages
8. polylingual   _____
9. panchromatic   sensitive to _____ colors
10. _____   of only one color
11. _____color   another name for the French flag, which is blue, white, and red in color
12. multilateral   having _____ sides; involving _____ governments
13. _____   involving two governments or organizations
14. _____lateral   affecting only one side or one government
15. semicolon   _____
16. semiannual   _____
17. _____   a room which is partially or half private
18. _____   half of a circle
19. _____   involving many nations
20. _____   all sides are the same

B. Match the prefixes *multi-, bi-, semi-,* and *equi-* with appropriate bases. In some cases there are two possibilities.

_____media	_____millionaire
_____monthly	_____purpose
_____skilled	_____cultural
_____vitamin	_____precious
_____circular	_____centenary
_____focal	_____distant
_____final	

C. From the following advertisement list the words with quantity prefixes. Try to define them.

BECOME A POLYGLOT
WITH OUR HOME UNIVERSITY LANGUAGE COURSES

With our easy-to-follow manuals you can become bilingual in your own home!! Our materials are the perfected versions of courses used by the Diplomatic Service Institute.

In addition to the tapes and instructional manual, you will receive a bimonthly multilingual newspaper with articles in French, Spanish, German, Italian, Russian, Mandarin, Swahili, and Japanese.

Our courses take the monotony out of language learning!

	Word	*Meaning*
1.	_____	_____
2.	_____	_____
3.	_____	_____
4.	_____	_____
5.	_____	_____

D. Read the following selection first for general comprehension. Then read it for details and highlight all the words with quantity prefixes.

Pan-Equatorian Organization Meets

TROPICA, West Equatoria (PP) The Pan-Equatorian Organization opened its semiannual meeting in Tropica today. On the agenda were proposals for a multimillion-dollar hydroelectric station to serve the tri-state area of Tropica, Savanna, and Occidentia, and a request for funding of a solar-powered station. The station would be located in Savanna, equidistant from Tropica and Occidentia.

A subcommittee on the development of the Pan-Equatorian transportation network presented a plan for a mono-rail service. The service, to be called Pan-Equatorian Transport, or PET for short, will be the first low-cost trans-

Dr. E. E. Sango advocates solar power for Savanna at Tropica meeting today.

Equatorian transportation system. This will help to unify the three nations on a multitude of levels in addition to providing transportation.

The subcommittee on multilingual issues pushed for a ruling that all official documents be trilingual: French, English, and the local language; and that universities now require all graduates to be bilingual – native language plus French or English. The education subcommittee unveiled plans for a Polytechnic Institute to be established in Savanna. The Institute will be the first cooperative educational venture undertaken by the three Equatorian nations.

The literacy subcommittee reported that the recent biennial survey of literacy in the three nations has shown that illiteracy has been reduced by 10 percent.

Discussion of bilateral trade agreements with the EEC was suspended until later.

Lesson 9

Cindy Speakwell • WPLA NEWSBREAK
Courtroom Drama Intensifies

CD track 9   Radio script page 99

TODAY'S
RADIO NEWS

Verb Prefixes and Suffixes: *en-, -en, be-, -ify, -ize, -ate*

One common way of showing that a word is a verb is to prefix or suffix it with **en.**
The meaning of **en** is, in general, to make or create. Sometimes it intensifies (makes stronger)
the meaning of the base.

en- is frequently prefixed to bases that are nouns or verbs:

> **enact** – to put something (especially a law) into action

If the base begins with a **b** or **p, en-** is spelled **em-:**

> **empower** – to give power to somebody

-en is frequently suffixed to adjectives of quality or dimension:

> **shorten** – to make shorter
> **sharpen** – to make sharper
> • *Note:* there is also the past participle inflection **-en**, which is a different kind of affix:
> **break – broke – broken**

be- as a prefix has an intensifying effect on the base form. It can also mean "to cause to ..."

> **belittle** – to speak of something as unimportant
> **becloud** – to cause something to be difficult to see or understand

-ify, -ate, and **-ize** are common verb suffixes that also mean, in general, "to make." There is
no easy way of knowing which suffix is attached to which base. The combinations have to be
memorized.

> • *Note:* in British English **-ize** is usually spelled **-ise**, although Americans also spell
> some words like *televise* with an **s**. Also note that a few words like **execute** or **prosecute**
> take a **-ute** suffix instead of **-ate**.

These **-ify, -ate,** and **-ize** verbs are easily turned into nouns by adding **-ion** and making a few
spelling changes. Note that **-ify** verbs usually add **-ication**.

> identify - identification   realize - realization
> investigate - investigation   contribute - contribution

Exercises

A. Some of the following bases are prefixed with **en-** or **em-**, and some are suffixed with **-en**. Try to use the correct affix.

soft	wide	trust	dorse
danger	close	loose	courage
able	gage	dure	counter
deep	bright	force	hance
ploy	weak	brace	gulf

B. Use the words below in the appropriate sentence.

beware	beclouded	behooves	belittle	betrayed
bereaved	bemoaned	bedeviled	bewildering	besieged

1. He _____ his friends and told the police where they were hiding.
2. This is a complex, _____ situation. I am confused.
3. The _____ parents _____ the loss of their only son.
4. Many problems have _____ the latest attempt to launch a satellite. The project may be canceled.
5. It _____ us to buy now. The price will never be lower.
6. _____ of the dog; it bites.
7. Don't _____ the idea unless you have a better one.
8. The city was _____ for months before it finally surrendered.
9. The issue was clear, but I'm afraid they have _____ it.

C. In these sentences use either the *-ate* or *-ize* verb suffix to make the verb form.

1. The demonstrators will _____ tomorrow.
2. The immigrants _____ mostly from the Far East.
3. The Nationalist party wants to _____ the steel industry.
4. As a dramatist, he _____ man's struggle with God and the devil.
5. Two assassins _____ the minister yesterday.
6. A private investigator will _____ the matter.
7. Negotiators have _____ a peaceful settlement.
8. If she's a university graduate, where did she _____ from?
9. The operators refused to _____ the equipment.
10. Terrorists have _____ the entire area.
11. We should never make this legal. If it is _____ , the problem will worsen.
12. At this time speculation is dangerous. Therefore, I refuse to _____ .

D. Put verb suffixes on the base forms below. Note that there is a word *certificate*, but it is a noun.

ident-	class-	capital-	simpl-	civil-	intens-
activ-	fals-	equal-	appropri-	ideal-	final-
loc-	uni-	toler-	differenti-	romantic-	cert-

E. Read the following article once through for general comprehension. Then read it again and highlight all the words with verb prefixes and suffixes. Note that although a word may have a verb affix, it may also have a noun suffix, following the verb affix. For example, *dramatization*, from *dramatize*. List all the words that contain a verb affix.

Courtroom Drama Intensifies

Doble calls Solo Drug King

Doble identifies Solo
Courtroom sketch by PR Moran

SAN TOMASO, Novo Mundo (PLN) —The trial of Juan Solo continued today in San Tomaso, as the prosecution, attempting to strengthen its case, brought forth a new witness to testify against Solo, who is accused of operating a huge drug empire that produces and distributes cocaine throughout central Caribea.

The witness, Julio Doble, identified Solo as the ringleader of a gang of drug dealers that for the past ten years has terrorized the provincial city of Los Gatos, located in the remote northeastern part of Andea. Doble, characterizing Solo as the "Andean Godfather," claimed that Solo had managed to centralize a chain of growers, processors, and distributors from his headquarters in Los Gatos.

Upon cross-examination by the defense, the witness, who had immigrated to Nova Mundo and become a naturalized citizen in 1986, admitted that he had falsified information on his naturalization papers and had covered up an arrest and conviction in 1981 for embezzling funds from the First Andean Bank, where he had been employed in the 1970's. Apparently, Doble also lost a large sum of money by speculating in real estate.

Bewildered by the defense's examination, the besieged witness also admitted that two years ago he had been investigated by the Novo Mundo Drug Enforcement Agency.

The defense appealed to the jury to recognize the witness as a questionable character, and stated that his testimony should be classified as simply that of "an informant whose only purpose is to betray Solo, a former ally in the drug world." Arguing that the defense was doing nothing more than trying to assassinate the character of the witness in order to frighten further witnesses, the federal attorney vowed to continue to prosecute the case with additional witnesses when the trial resumes tomorrow.

Lesson 10

Walter Conrad • WPLA EVENING NEWS
R. J. Lee, Territoria Leader, Dies
CD track 10   Radio script page 100

TODAY'S
RADIO NEWS

Noun Suffixes: *-ance/-ence, -ity, -hood, -ship, -ness*

Suffixes are attached to the end of a base, and they do two things. They carry some meaning, and they show that they are a noun, verb, adjective, or adverb. For example, in Lesson 3 we saw that the **-er** suffix means "one who," and it also shows that the word is a noun.

In this lesson we will look at some other suffixes that form nouns. (In other lessons we will study adjective, adverb, and verb suffixes.) In general, the noun suffixes in this lesson mean the "condition, state of being, or quality" of the base they are affixed to. For example, if you have *security*, your condition is *secure*. Often when these suffixes are affixed to a base ending in a vowel, the final vowel is either changed or dropped, as it is in *insurance*.

-ance/-ence has these variant forms: *-ancy/-ency/-acy.*

> **insure + ance** = insurance
> **intelligent + ence** = intelligence
> **president + ency** = presidency
> **occupant + ancy** = occupancy
> **democrat + acy** = democracy

-ity is occasionally spelled *-ety.*

> **safe + ity** = safety   **soci + ity** = society

-hood can mean "condition, state, or quality," but it can also mean "a group of."

> **state + hood** = statehood - the condition of being a state
> **neighbor + hood** = neighborhood - a place where a group of neighbors live
> **brother + hood** = brotherhood - either a group of brothers or the quality of being like brothers

-ship, in addition to meaning "condition, state, or quality," can also mean "status, rank, or office."

> **leader + ship** = leadership (quality)
> **professor + ship** = professorship (rank)

-ness means "condition, state, or quality," and it is frequently suffixed to adjectives that already have an adjective suffix.

> **kind + ness** = kindness - the quality of being kind
> **careful + ness** = carefulness - the quality of being careful
> **divisive + ness** = divisiveness - the quality of being divisive
> **sleepy + ness** = sleepiness - the state of being sleepy
> **drunken + ness** = drunkenness - the condition or state of being drunk

Exercises

A. Rewrite the following words to see if you can guess which affix to use: **-ance, -ence, -ancy, -ency, -acy**.

intelligent	_____	assist	_____
assure	_____	dissident	_____
president	_____	democrat	_____
conspire	_____	insist	_____
disturb	_____	prefer	_____
candidate	_____	illiterate	_____
agent	_____	differ	_____
disappear	_____	confer	_____
resident	_____	independent	_____

B. Add the suffix **-ity** to these words (watch the spelling) and use the word in one of the sentences.

secure	_____	active	_____
captive	_____	equal	_____
similar	_____	safe	_____
familiar	_____	human	_____

1. There is a great _____ between the flags of Australia and New Zealand.

2. When will _____ ever achieve universal peace?

3. I have no _____ with that subject.

4. The prisoner was kept in _____ for two years.

5. "Our goal is _____ and brotherhood," he said.

6. _____ is important in the workplace. Accidents reduce productivity.

7. Observers reported that there was no unusual _____ along the border today.

8. _____ will be tight when the President visits the provincial capital.

C. Fill in the blanks with a noun form of the underlined adjective, using **-ness**.

1. The rate of change has been steady.
   Its _____ is very assuring.

2. The comments are unworthy of response.
   The _____ of your comments is disappointing.

3. His response was correct.
   The _____ of his response was not surprising.

4. The night was <u>still</u>.

The _____ of the night was pleasant.

5. You are very <u>kind</u>.

Your _____ is much appreciated.

6. The situation was <u>hopeless</u>.

The _____ of the situation was obvious.

7. One <u>careless</u> act can create a disaster.

The disaster was caused by _____.

8. She was trying to be <u>helpful</u>.

Her _____ was sincere.

9. Don't be <u>foolish</u>.

They won't tolerate your _____.

10. He was always very <u>busy</u> but <u>careful</u>.

His _____ helped him build a good _____.

D. Add either *-ship* or *-hood*.

1. He has citizen_____ in two countries.

2. Alaska achieved state_____ in 1959.

3. We live in a quiet neighbor_____ .

4. Her leader_____ was inspiring.

5. Throughout his child_____ he was often sick.

6. I am against all forms of censor_____ .

7. The craftsman_____ in this jewelry is unequaled anywhere.

8. This country has lived under a dictator_____ for too many years.

9. This union is called the Brother_____ of Mine Workers.

10. Nehru's statesman_____ earned him the respect of people everywhere.

E. Read the following article and highlight the words with the noun suffixes we have studied in this lesson.

Leader of Independence Movement Dies

HONG CITY, Territoria (PLN) –

Condolences and tributes continued to pour into the capital of Territoria, as the citizens began an official three-day mourning period for the death of R. J. Lee, who passed away peacefully at his residence Tuesday morning.

Born and brought up in a poverty-stricken neighborhood in the provincial city of Interioria, Lee first gained national recognition when he led the Brotherhood of Mine Workers in a successful strike and a series of protests against expatriate mine ownership.

In the 1930s he served his political apprenticeship as a District Representative to the legislature during the colonial administration. His political experiences, however, turned him against the government, and together with W. W. Hong, he founded the Unity Party and began to develop its policy of civil disobedience.

In the closing years of the colonial administration, Lee came into prominence as a leader of the independence movement, and in 1955, as a champion of democracy, he announced his candidacy for Prime Minister with his now famous "Equality and Opportunity" address, delivered at the closing session of the National Legislature.

Elected as Prime Minister of Territoria, Lee led the country in its first few years of nationhood. Although noted for his fairness and his tolerance of minority opinion, he was frequently criticized by the independent press for operating an undeclared dictatorship.

In 1962 he was elected to the presidency of Territoria. As President, Lee achieved an international reputation for his statesmanship and his life-long adherence to nonviolence. He helped establish the Annual Conference of Nonaligned Nations.

Over the next few days official delegations from dozens of countries will assemble in the capital to attend the final ceremonies for the ex-President. He will be buried Friday in the National Cemetery.

Lesson 11

 Maria Ventura • WPLA The Morning Show
Assassination Investigation
CD track 11   Radio script page 101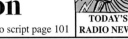
TODAY'S RADIO NEWS

Noun Suffixes: *-ion, -ment, -ism, -age, -dom*

In the previous lesson we studied noun suffixes that refer to condition, state, or quality. The suffixes in this lesson are similar but can also have an "active" meaning.

-ion, which usually indicates "an act, process, or condition," is sometimes spelled *-tion, -sion, -ation,* and *-ition*.

> **act + ion** = action
> **nutri + tion** = nutrition
> **suspen + sion** = suspension
> **domin + ation** = domination
> **compet + ition** = competition

-ment, which can mean "action, product, or state," is a common suffix.

> **govern + ment** = government

-ism can refer to action: **terror + ism** = terrorism
or to qualities: **hero + ism** = heroism
or to a doctrine or principle: **commun + ism** = communism

-age can mean "an action or condition": **marry + age** = marriage
or "a collection or mass": **post + age** = postage

-dom is the only suffix in this group that doesn't refer to action. It is not a common suffix, and it usually means "a field of interest or action."

> **king + dom** = kingdom

In a few cases it can refer to a condition:

> **free + dom** = freedom

Exercises

A. We have seen one form or another of all these **-ion** suffixed words in previous lessons. All of these nouns can be changed into verbs. Write the verb form next to the noun.

investigation	_____	pollution	_____
location	_____	disruption	_____
prevention	_____	rejection	_____
prosecution	_____	indication	_____
collision	_____	conclusion	_____
confirmation	_____	organization	_____
identification	_____	presentation	_____
demonstration	_____	provision	_____
acclamation	_____	graduation	_____
contribution	_____	cooperation	_____
immigration	_____	recognition	_____
opposition	_____	election	_____
eruption	_____	operation	_____
administration	_____	explosion	_____

What did you notice about nouns that end with **-sion**?

B. Most of the words in this list take a **-ment** suffix, but a few do not. Add the **-ment** suffix to the appropriate words, and put an X beside the words that do not take a **-ment** suffix.

appoint	_____	develop	_____
announce	_____	require	_____
expect	_____	contribute	_____
manage	_____	compose	_____
govern	_____	establish	_____
state	_____	move	_____
criticize	_____		

C. All of the **-ism** words below can be found in one form or another in readings 1-8. A person who is involved in an **-ism** is usually an **-ist**. In the list below, only two "people" words do not have an **-ist** ending. Can you find them?

terrorism	_____	conservatism	_____
tourism	_____	nationalism	_____
idealism	_____	socialism	_____
activism	_____	criticism	_____
capitalism	_____	colonialism	_____
classicism	_____	opportunism	_____

D. Complete the following sentences using **-dom** and **-age** suffixes.
Most of the words will require **-age**, which is much more common than **-dom**.

1. The ship was wrecked. Some of the _____ came ashore.

2. All the media covered the event. The _____ was very complete.

3. They shot many feet of film. The film _____ was examined closely.

4. She is a star. She achieved _____ at an early age.

5. The river was polluted by sewers. The _____ came from the city.

6. It cost a lot to post the letter. The _____ was very high.

7. We are free. We have _____ at last!

8. It is the same size as a pack of cigarettes. It comes in a small _____.

9. An auto can carry things. It used to be called a horseless _____.

10. The freezer broke and the meat spoiled. The restaurant was not insured against food _____.

11. He is a martyr. He achieved _____ by dying for his country.

12. They were bored by the speech. Their _____ was easy to see.

13. The two movie stars were married last year. Their _____ lasted only a year.

14. He had three bags. The _____ allowance was only two bags. (He had too much luggage.)

15. Some articles will be broken. You should allow for 10% _____.

16. She's a stock broker. Her business is a _____.

E. Read the following article first for general comprehension. Then read it more closely and highlight all the words with suffixes we have studied in this lesson.

HAMAD III, LATE KING OF BURANIA

Assassination Investigation

MIRAGE, Burania (PLN) The normally peaceful Monarchy of Burania is slowly returning to business as usual after the shocking assassination last Tuesday of King Hamad III. Shops and offices that remained closed yesterday began to open today as the government issued a declaration that the administration of the Kingdom would not be disrupted by terrorism.

Although positive identification of the assassin has not been made, an announcement from the Ministry of Information has tentatively linked the assassin, who was shot and killed on the spot by the the king's bodyguards, to the little-known Burania Freedom Fighters faction.

Meanwhile, an anonymous phone caller, claiming to be a member of the outlawed ODN (Organization for Democratic Nationalism) praised the dead assassin saying, "He has attained martyrdom, and others will follow in his footsteps."

The Central Intelligence Department's investigation of the murder is continuing under the direction of Major General Adam. According to Adam, studies of television film footage have revealed the possible presence of a second assassin who may have fired a rifle from the rooftop of the Hotel Elegan. The figure on the rooftop lends credence to the speculation that the King may have been hit by a bullet a split second before the terrorist bomb exploded in his open carriage. The Monarch, who was being driven to a reception at the Palace, was apparently killed by the explosion of the package bomb hurled by the assailant. The vehicle's wreckage is being examined for the presence of the rifle slugs, and it is expected that the results of an autopsy on the King will be released later today.

A statement this morning from the King's son, Prince Mahad, appealed to the citizens of Burania to remain calm. "Their aim is disruption and anarchy," he said, referring to the murderers, "but we must work for the continuation of my father, the king's, peaceful and progressive rule."

Lesson 12

Adjective Suffixes: *-able, -less, -al, -en*

The suffix *-able* means "can or able to ..." and the suffix *-less* means "to be without or lacking."

-able is also spelled *-ible*. There are no simple rules to know which spelling is used. You may need to consult a dictionary. In general, however, bases that are complete words add *-able*. Also notice that if the word ends in *e*, sometimes the *e* is dropped. If the word ends in *-ate*, the *-ate* is usually dropped and *-able* is added.

> **return + able** = returnable – can be returned
> **incred + ible** = incredible – cannot be believed
> **believ(e) + able** = believable – can be believed
> **demonstr(ate) + able** = demonstrable – can be demonstrated

-less means "Without."
> **hopeless** – without hope

-al means "related to or characterized by."
> **political** – relating to politics

-en means "made of or resembling." Be careful that you don't confuse this suffix with the past participle inflection (break, broke, broken) or the verb suffix *-en* *(sharpen, widen, lengthen).*
> **wooden** - made of wood

Exercises

A. It is not easy to choose between *-able* and *-ible*. Try adding the suffix to these bases.

believe	_____	response	_____
permiss-	_____	tolerate	_____
receive	_____	reason	_____
question	_____	predict	_____
advise	_____	defense	_____
poss-	_____	consider	_____
accept	_____	cred-	_____
measure	_____	manage	_____
operate	_____	defend	_____

B. Create a new word using the italicized word in the following sentences:

1. He is a very ordinary person. It's not easy to *recognize* him. He's not easily _____.

2. Although the noise is rather loud I can *tolerate* it. It is _____.

3. Natural gas has no *odor* and no *color* and cannot be *detected*. Since it is _____ and _____, an odor has been added to make it _____.

4. Everyone *likes* her; she has a _____ personality.

5. Thank you for a very _____ evening. We *enjoyed* ourselves a lot.

6. This card table is _____. If you *collapse* the legs it can be stored behind the door.

7. A discussion or meeting that produced no results or *fruit* can be called _____.

8. This plastic tube can be bent or *flexed* easily; it is _____.

9. There is no *hope* for this patient; his situation is _____.

10. At one time it was the *fashion*, or it was _____, for men to wear ruffled shirts.

C. Add the appropriate adjectival suffix to each word and keep in mind that those with the suffix **-en** generally mean "made of," while those ending in **-al** mean "related to or characterized by ..."

1. It is just an old wood_____ box, but it is special to me because my grandfather made it when he was just a boy.

2. The doctor recommended that the patient be hospitalized since he was showing suicid_____ tendencies.

3. A dentist is also called an or_____ surgeon since his work is related to the mouth.

4. This course is not required; it is option_____.

5. There were many colorful flor_____ arrangements at the ceremony.

6. The dining room table is egg-shaped, or ov_____.

7. She survived the cold because she was wearing heavy wool_____ clothes and a therm_____ jacket.

8. This is a gold_____ opportunity!

9. The reception is form_____ ; you should wear a suit and tie.

10. The Indians made good use of their environment to produce their everyday necessities such as earth_____ware pottery.

D. Match the adjectives with the most appropriate nouns. (Suggestion: Choose a noun. Then read the list of adjectives and find the most appropriate one.)

1. tropical _____   a. animal
2. woolen _____   b. table
3. classical _____   c. action
4. defenseless _____   d. job
5. legal _____   e. island
6. golden _____   f. analysis
7. thankless _____   g. music
8. unbelievable _____   h. ring
9. wooden _____   i. sweater
10. financial _____   j. story

E. Read the following article first for general comprehension. Then read it more closely and highlight all the words with the suffixes we have studied in this lesson.

First Annual World Series

HIROSHIMA, Japan (PLN) The sound of wooden bats smacking baseballs is over for the year. And what a year! In a tense but highly enjoyable series of playoff games during the last two weeks, it all ended yesterday when the Hiroshima Carp made an incredible 6-5 come-back against the Washington Nationals in the final inning and took home the golden trophy as the true World Champions of Baseball.

The quarterfinals, starting two weeks ago, featured some unhittable pitching and unbelievable fielding. Even the winless Kansas City Royals played flawless baseball, but unable to hit well, they lost all five games by just one run in each game.

Just three days ago in the semifinals, the Cuban National team lost to Washington in tropical Havana 6-4, and on the other side of the world, Hiroshima defeated Taipei in extra innings, 3-2.

The stage was set for the thrilling final game. Ahead 5 - 0 in the ninth inning, the Nationals seemed unstoppable behind the brilliant pitching of Lefty Jackson. With one last chance, the Carp's situation seemed hopeless. But the fearless Carp rallied, and the apparently tireless Lefty's effortless pitching fell apart. Suzuki and Hiromi walked to begin the inning. Matsui, hitless in three previous attempts, reached on an error by the usually reliable second base-man, Jimmy Cooper. In trouble, Jackson gave up hits to Kimura and Yagata. With two runs in, Manager Billy Green brought in his ace stopper, Bullet Bill Robinson, to pitch to Matsui. With one swing Matsui sent the ball high over the wall, and the impossible became believable. Hiroshima 6, Washington 5.

Quarterfinal Results

East	Won	Lost	South	Won	Lost	West	Won	Lost	Far East	Won	Lost
Washington	5	0	Cuba	4	1	St. Louis	4	1	Hiroshima	5	0
Toronto	4	1	Venezuela	3	2	Monterey	3	2	Seoul	3	2
Boston	3	2	Dominican Rep	3	2	Calgary	3	2	Shanghai	3	2
Cincinnati	2	3	Panama	2	3	Mexico City	3	2	Manila	2	3
Atlanta	1	4	Colombia	2	3	Los Angeles	2	3	Sydney	1	4
Chicago	0	5	Puerto Rico	1	4	Kansas City	0	5	Taipei	1	4

Semifinals

Washington 6, Cuba 4   Hiroshima 3, St. Louis 2

Lesson 13

Adjective Suffixes: *-ful, -y, ous, -ary*

Like the adjective suffixes **-able** and **-less,** the suffix **-ful** is easy to define. It means that something is "full of or filled with." It can also have a more general meaning of "having the quality of, or the tendency to ..." The suffixes **-y** and **-ous** are similar in meaning to **-ful.** Here are some examples of **-ful**, **-y**, **-ous**:

peaceful	dirty	famous
successful	cloudy	dangerous
faithful	salty	various
purposeful	sleepy	serious

> • *Note:* There is another **-y** suffix which is used to mean something small or dear. For example: **kitty, daddy, mommy.**

The **-ary** suffix means "connected with" or "engaged in." Remember that there is also a noun suffix **-ary,** which is also spelled **-ory** (see Lesson 5). Here are some words with **-ary** as an adjective suffix: **ordinary, secondary, budgetary.**

Exercises

A. Give a short explanation of the following phrases.

migratory birds _____

respiratory illness _____

purposeful activity _____

dangerous weapon _____

scandalous affair _____

monotonous sound _____

helpful advice _____

skillful politician _____

snowy weather _____

silky fabric _____

starry sky _____

B.   Provide an appropriate suffix for the underlined words. Check your work in the dictionary.

1. Economists are hope_____ that the current fiscal year will end with a lower rate
   of inflation than last year.

2. Conservative investors are wary of speculation and prefer to use caution or to be cauti_____ .

3. The development of communication systems has brought revolution_____ changes to the
   21st century world.

4. He is an expert chef; he learned his culin_____ skills at the best restaurants in Paris.

5. Please be very care_____ not to wake the baby when you enter.

6. To prevent the spread of disease we must take precaution_____ measures.

7. Measles is an infecti_____ disease.

8. If you want to lose weight you should avoid greas_____ and starch_____ foods.

9. It is too fogg_____ to drive right now.

10. She owns a luxuri_____ house at the seaside.

C.   Transform the following words into adjectives by applying the correct suffixes:

ridicule	prime
oil	faith
thank	envy
scare	ice
greed	melody
ambition	pearl
thought	second
inflation	purpose
fiction	vision

What did you notice about the spelling of words that end with **-y** to which the suffix **-ous** is attached?

D.   Many **-y** suffixes are used to describe weather conditions.
     Circle the "weather " words in the list below.

snowy	grassy	sunny
stony	foggy	rocky
windy	dusty	sandy
muddy	icy	rainy
chilly	hazy	smoggy
salty	smoky	cloudy
milky	hilly	misty

E. Read the following story for general comprehension. Then highlight the *-ful*, *-y*, *-ous*, and *-ary* words.

Disastrous Earthquake in Kosharam

KASHKAR, Kosharam (PLN) A disastrous earthquake in the mountainous region of Kosharam has killed hundreds and completely destroyed many villages built on the rocky slopes of the Altaya Mountains. Survivors are staying in temporary housing provided by voluntary relief organizations.

The primary shock waves from the powerful earthquake registered 7.2 on the Richter scale. It occurred Sunday morning when most people were at home. Hundreds of buildings collapsed, killing or trapping the unwary residents. Most of the ordinary houses had been built long before the establishment of the Regulatory Building Commission, and therefore they did not have sturdy, earthquake-proof foundations.

Several poor neighborhoods in the hilly terrain surrounding the city of Kashkar were destroyed by landslides. Dangerous landslide conditions had been created by the previous week's exceptionally rainy weather, and the quake's first jolt caused the sandy, rain-soaked soil to slip down the hillsides.

Secondary shock waves were also reported to have struck the region Monday evening, but fortunately no disastrous results were recorded.

Generous donations have been pouring in from thoughtful citizens everywhere. The parliamentary session opened Monday with a moment of silence to honor those who had perished, which was followed by an immediate resolution to grant financial assistance and help from the military forces to the stricken region.

Lesson 14

 Maria Ventura • WPLA The Morning Show
Dramatic Rescue at Island Park
CD track 14   Radio script page 104 **TODAY'S RADIO NEWS**

Adjective Suffixes: *-ish, -ic, -ive*

These suffixes are frequently used to mean "having a tendency to, related to, or characteristic of" the base to which they are joined.

> **reddish brown** - a brown color that has some red
> **childish behavior** - behavior (in an adult) that is like a child's
> **destructive storm** - a storm that destroys things (causes destruction)
> **economic report** - a report that is related to the economy

- *Note:* Be careful of the difference between *economic* and *economical*, which means "not expensive to operate."

Exercises

A. Try to guess the right suffix. There are four *-ic*, four *-ish*, and three *-ive* suffixes in the sentences below.

1. The soldier was given a medal for his hero_____ behavior.

2. She has a schizophren_____ personality.

3. We appreciate construct_____ comments but not destruct_____ ones.

4. Her eyes are brown_____.

5. The comedian's boy_____, com_____ behavior makes people laugh.

6. No one can say that he is self_____; he always puts others first.

7. The artist's creat_____ work was not appreciated in her lifetime.

8. How could anyone make such a fool_____ mistake?!!

9. People with ulcers should not eat acid_____ fruits.

Answers for Lesson 14 on page 85   **Lesson 14: Adjective Suffixes:** *-ish, -ic, -ive* • **47**

B.   Use the list below to fill in the blanks in the sentences.

collective	fantastic	brackish	organic
sluggish	metallic	conclusive	fortyish
girlish	microscopic	geometric	

1.   The aluminum pot gave the coffee a _____ taste.

2.   In the hot, sweltering summer temperatures, we were too _____ to play any active sports.

3.   _____ organisms are very, very small.

4.   The judge said there was not enough _____ evidence to find the defendant guilty.

5.   Don't let her _____ appearance fool you; she is really _____.

6.   Even though centuries old, the Turkish kilims' _____ designs fit in well with many modern decors.

7.   Believing that synthetic chemical fertilizers are harmful, _____ farmers use only natural fertilizers.

8.   The view from the mountaintop is _____.

9.   Water that is somewhat salty is _____ water.

10. _____ bargaining enabled the workers to negotiate for better working conditions.

C.   Complete the following with an appropriate adjective. Partial spellings have been given to help you. Use your dictionary if necessary.

1.   Her eyes are not really a deep or pure blue; they are more of a gr_____ish blue.

2.   The de_____ive storm destroyed many buildings.

3.   A woman who is not beautiful but who attracts attention can be called att_____ive.

4.   If I tickle or touch you in sensitive places and you laugh, you are t_____lish.

5.   Many people do not believe in UFO's (unidentified flying objects) because there

     is no scien_____c evidence of their existence.

6.   If you want to emphasize something, you can underline it or use ital_____script to make

     it stand out.

7.   Although inches, feet, and yards are still commonly used in the USA, the met_____
     system is taught in the public school and is often used in science and technology.

8.   To straighten the child's crooked teeth the dentist recommended correct_____braces.

9.   To take this course you must have a bas_____ knowledge of the principles of accounting.

D. Give the noun and verb forms of the following adjectives.

ADJECTIVE   NOUN   VERB

dramatic   drama _____   dramatize _____

magnetic   _____   _____

telephonic   _____   _____

systematic   _____   _____

explosive   _____   _____

creative   _____   _____

defensive   _____   _____

conclusive   _____   _____

disruptive   _____   _____

progressive   _____   _____

decisive   _____   _____

productive   _____   _____

E. The names of some nationalities and languages end with an *-ish* suffix and can be used as nouns or adjectives. Can you name some?

_____   _____   _____

_____   _____   _____

_____   _____   _____

_____   _____   _____

_____   _____   _____

F. Read the following passage first for general comprehension. Then read it for details and highlight all the *-ish*, *-ic*, and *-ive* suffixes.

Dramatic Rescue at Island Park

Eli Sharp with Metropol pilot Chuck Friendly

PLACIDBORO, Wabbassetshire (PLN)

The sleepy Wabasset River town Placidboro, usually an idyllic spot year-round, was awakened from its slumber Sunday morning to find that massive ice blocks had broken loose from the river's frozen surface. The broken ice flowed downriver to Island Park, where it piled up and began a relentless destruction of the island. Fortunately, no one was hurt, although damage to property was extensive.

Eli Sharp, caretaker of Island Park Casino, had been stranded on the island since the ice began breaking up at around 2:00 Sunday morning. With much of the island covered by thick chunks of ice, Sharp was forced to take refuge on the roof of the casino building.

Called to the scene by Sharp's frantic wife, the Placidboro Public Safety Department attempted to rescue Sharp by motorboat, but despite the heroic efforts of the crew, the normally sluggish river was choked with floating ice, and they were unable to reach the island.

Within an hour, however, a police helicopter from nearby Metropol picked Sharp from the roof of the casino in a dramatic rescue operation, just as the destructive force of water and ice began to destroy the casino. Sharp, unharmed but slightly feverish from exposure to the cold, was transferred to the hospital for observation.

Casino owner Frank Chance looked on helplessly as his classic wooden structure was slowly destroyed. Asked if he would rebuild, Chance replied that for the moment he was simply grateful for the unselfish efforts of the rescuers, and that he was thankful that his trusted employee Sharp was alive.

Chance went on to praise the decisive action of Police Chief Standish and the rescuers. "They were terrific," said Chance.

Lesson 15

Walter Conrad • WPLA Evening News
Climate Change Definitely Here?
CD track 15   Radio script page 105

TODAY'S
RADIO NEWS

Adverb Suffixes: *-ly, -ward, -wise*

The most active and common adverb suffix is **-ly.** It can be added to a long list of words (mostly adjectives) to make them into adverbs, words that modify adjectives or verbs. The adverb ending is often added to words that already have a suffix, but notice that the adverb suffix always comes last. Note the order of affixes in **internationally**, which has four affixes:

inter-	nat	-ion	-al	-ly
prefix	base	noun suffix	adjective suffix	adverb suffix

There are some spelling problems with **-ly.**

1. In a word that ends in a **y** preceded by a consonant, change the **y** to **i**:
    happy + ly = happily

2. In an adjective that ends in **-ble, -ple, -tle, -dle,** drop the **-le:**
    possible + ly = possibly

3. With adjectives that end in **-ic,** add **-al** before **-ly:**
    basic + ly = basically

4. With adjectives ending in "silent" **-e,** keep the **-e:**
    extreme + ly = extremely

5. With adjectives ending in **l,** keep the **l:**
    careful + ly = carefully

   • *Note:* A few words suffixed with **-ly** are normally adjectives: **lively, friendly, neighborly, lovely, lonely**.

-ward is usually suffixed to words of direction. The list is short. Note that an **-s** can be added to the end of most of these words with no change in meaning.

toward(s)	**backward(s)**
downward(s)	**forward(s)**
upward(s)	**homeward(s)**
inward(s)	**onward(s)**
outward(s)	**skyward**

-wise is suffixed to a few words to make them into adverbs:

lengthwise   **clockwise**   **crosswise**

It is quite common nowadays to add the *-wise* suffix to nouns. However, this is not yet a fully acceptable practice. This adverbial expression means "pertaining to ... "
For example: *Moneywise*, we've got to be careful. We're almost broke!

moneywise   **marketwise**   **timewise**   **taxwise**

> • *Note:* The adverbs *likewise* and *otherwise* are fully acceptable words, meaning similarly and differently.

Exercises

A. Below are some adjectives that we have seen before. Rewrite each word with the *-ly* suffix, spelling carefully.

federal	_____	responsible	_____
automatic	_____	national	_____
apparent	_____	appropriate	_____
intelligent	_____	immediate	_____
normal	_____	peaceful	_____
political	_____	successful	_____
ideal	_____	clever	_____
environmental	_____	independent	_____
conservative	_____	democratic	_____
illegal	_____	fair	_____
financial	_____	progressive	_____
steady	_____	secure	_____

B. Write the adverb form in the following sentences.

1. His progress is steady. He is progressing _____.

2. Active participation is necessary. Please participate _____.

3. She's always fair. She treats people _____.

4. Be sure it is secure. Tie it _____.

5. He is a successful businessman. He manages his business _____.

6. I will take a conservative view. I will act _____.

7. The situation is normal. Everything is proceeding _____.

8. She is known everywhere in the nation. She is a _____ known person.

9. The problem is apparent. _____ this is the problem.

10. We are concerned about the environment. We are _____ concerned citizens.

11. Their reaction was immediate. They reacted _____.

12. Let's seek a peaceful solution. Let's solve the problem _____.

13. That was an illegal act. He did it _____.

14. It's an automatic rifle. It fires _____.

15. We need an appropriate response. We need to respond _____.

C. Match each phrase on the left with a phrase on the right.

1. Illegally printed money is _____   a. in a good location.

2. A democratically ruled nation is _____   b. interesting and entertaining.

3. A financially independent person is _____ c. an important point in time.

4. An ideally situated home is _____   d. worthless.

5. A federally funded project is _____   e. usually peaceful.

6. A steadily increasing debt is _____   f. for the purpose of maintaining power.

7. A normally idyllic place is _____   g. a country with free elections.

8. A cleverly told story is _____   h. not in need of money.

9. A politically motivated action is _____   i. growing larger every day.

10. A critically decisive moment is _____   j. one which receives government money.

D. Use the words below in the sentences. Use each word only once.

lengthwise	downward	skyward	inward
otherwise	forward	outward	homeward
toward	backward		

1. The price of the food is dropping. It's going _____.

2. The rocket roared _____.

3. The city is slowly expanding _____.

4. Place it the long way. Place it _____.

5. We're not making progress. We're going _____.

6. Most of the traffic leaving the city in the evening is _____ bound to the suburbs.

7. We should leave now. _____, we'll be late.

8. We are moving _____ a solution.

9. We were moving _____. Then we came to a complete stop.

10. The psychiatrist said, "I want you to look _____ and get in touch with your real feelings."

E. Read the following article quickly and completely. Then read it again and highlight the adverb suffixes.

A

Climate Change Definitely Here to Stay?

NOVA ARKANSK, Eurovia (PLN) At the conclusion of a three-day conference in Nova Arkansk, an internationally known group of environmental scientists released a dramatically worded statement on the "greenhouse" effect. The scientists issued a warning that the increasing use of fossil fuels and the release of chemicals into the atmosphere is leading invariably to steadily rising temperature levels and climatic changes that will create enormous disruptions globally, including a rise in ocean levels and flooding of coastal areas. They emphasized that the problem is absolutely real and unquestionably getting worse.

The report also stressed the negative effects, politically and economically, on densely populated coastal regions, especially those of Asia and the Pacific region. Low-lying islands may be partially or even completely inundated, forcing thousands of islanders to leave. Mainland coastal areas, which would also be severely affected, contain nearly one-third of the world's population.

Additionally, much of the world's great rice-growing area in Asia could be drastically affected as increasingly brackish water would be devastating to the variety of rice currently grown in these areas.

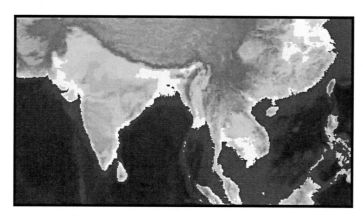

Coastal lands in Asia (shown in white) that might be permanently flooded if the sea level were to rise by 80 meters. Millions of people would be displaced in India, Southeast Asia, Indonesia, Japan, the Philippines, and China. Irreplaceable agricultural lands would be lost, causing wide-spread famine.

The report shows conclusively that burning of fossil fuels directly results in an increase in carbon dioxide. The increase in carbon dioxide, which traps the sun's rays in the lower atmosphere, indirectly causes the temperature increase.

On the one hand, with more carbon dioxide in the atmosphere, agricultural productivity will increase significantly. Carbon dioxide enhances photosynthesis in green plants and decreases moisture requirements. Accordingly, some nations may benefit from climatic changes; others, principally developing nations, will be sorely pressed to cope with the changes. Agricultural conditions worldwide will almost certainly be significantly altered. Environmental and economic systems will be disrupted.

The scientists called for a multinational effort by developing and developed nations to work together immediately toward a meaningful solution. The report concluded by stating that priority must be given to reducing the use of fossil fuels, and preserving and expanding forests which absorb carbon dioxide. "We must look forward," the scientists said, "and keep our vision straight ahead to the future. We cannot delay another year, or civilization in the 21st century will slip backward into turmoil and chaos." Some of the scientists issued a separate statement saying that solving the problem is not only urgent, it may be too late.

Map drawn by Tim Osborn, Climatic Research Unit, UEA, Norwich, U.K. Copyright © 2014 Tim Osborn.

Lesson 16

Position Prefixes: *pre-, post-, inter-, intro-/intra-, extro-/extra-, contra-, ante-*

In this lesson we will look at prefixes that modify the base word by giving information about the location of the base in space or time.

Preposition is a good example to help you remember this group of prefixes.

Pre- and *post-* are very common prefixes that mean "before" and "after." These prefixes can be attached to many bases: A hyphen is used if the combination is somewhat unusual, or if the base begins with a capital letter. And if the base begins with the letter *e*, the *pre-* prefix is hyphenated.

> **pretrial** – before the trial (in time)
> **postwar** – after the war (in time)

inter- means "between."

> **interstate** – between the states

intra- and *intro-* are different spellings of the same prefix which means "in" or "within."

> **intrastate** – within a state

extra- and *extro-* are the opposite of intra-/intro-, and they mean "outside."

> **extraterrestrial** – outside the earth (Remember E.T.?)

contra- means against or opposite (also see Lessons 7 and 20).

> **contradance** – a dance in which the couples are opposite each other in a line

Finally, there is another prefix that means "before": *ante-*. This is sometimes confused with *anti-,* which means "against" (See Lesson 7). This is not a common prefix, but here are a few examples:

> **antecedent** – something that comes before
> **anteroom** – a waiting room
> **ante meridian** (a.m.) – before the sun reaches the meridian at noon

Answers for Lesson 16 on page 85

Exercises

A. Some bases normally take a *pre-* prefix, some normally take a *post-* prefix, and some can take either. Try to put the following bases in the right column.

caution	graduate	war	-judice
-pone	colonial	-dict	-natal (birth)
view	-pare (get ready)	trial	-vent
school	mature	pay	-scription
historic	Moslem		script (p.s.)

PRE-	POST-	PRE- and/or POST-

B. Use one of the words in the list below in each of the sentences. Use each word only once.

international	intersection	interview
intermediate	intermission	interpreter
interstate	interrupt	intercollegiate

1. I saw her during the _____ at the concert.

2. When you apply for a job, you often go for an _____ .

3. The United Nations is an _____ organization.

4. I wish you wouldn't _____ me when I am talking.

5. She works as a French - English _____ .

6. She is studying German at the _____ level.

7. The store is located at the _____ of Main Street and 3rd Avenue.

8. _____ basketball is played by university and college teams.

9. This _____ highway goes through six states.

C. Read the following sentences and give a definition for the underlined word.

1. He participated in many extracurricular activities when he was at the university: football, debating club, political science club, and university newspaper.

   Extracurricular = _____

2. Although he didn't play intercollegiate football, he did play in the intramural league. I think he played for his dormitory team.

   intramural = _____

3. The Starship Enterprise was designed for extragalactic travel. It often travels beyond the "Milky Way" galaxy.

   extragalactic = _____

4. She is very friendly – a real extrovert. He is a shy introvert.

   extrovert = _____

   introvert = _____

5. The patient could not eat. We had to feed him intravenously.

   intravenously = _____

6. It was an extraordinary story – front-page news.

   extraordinary = _____

7. Meditation and yoga are forms of introspection.

   introspection = _____

8. Some people believe in ESP (extrasensory perception) and mind reading.

   extrasensory = _____

9. Senator Hawk contradicted Senator Dove and said he disagreed with Dove's proposal.

   contradict = _____

D. Read the following article quickly and completely. Then read it again, highlighting position prefixes.

FTBU Protests ICPC's Intracoastal Beach Conference

INTRACOASTAL BEACH, Pelagia (PLN) Today the International Committee for Population Control (ICPC) announced that its plans for an intercontinental conference next week on birth control here at Intracoastal Beach will not be postponed. This past week, thousands of protestors have tried to prevent the ICPC members from attending a pre-conference workshop.

Dr. J. P. Ahmedi, in a recent interview with the media, said that the ICPC will not allow demonstrators to interfere with the extraordinarily important issue of controlling population growth. According to Dr. Ahmedi, "Our work is dedicated to insuring that human life will continue. We work not for ourselves, but for posterity. This issue precedes all others in importance." Ahmedi's Committee continues to support the worldwide distribution of contraceptives.

W. W. Stoppit, top right, and family   MJ Studios

Later, on a local television station, W. W. Stoppit, in a post-demonstration interview, was quoted as saying, "We are prepared to interrupt the proceedings of the conference." Speaking through an interpreter, Stoppit claimed that birth control is only a "prelude to mind control." The Free to Breed Union (FTBU) plans a post-workshop rally in the capital to introduce an extravagant effort for new and tough laws banning contraceptives as well as extramarital sex. When asked about his public support of his lesbian daughter, Stoppit insisted that there was nothing contradictory in his strong support of "Family Values," and "Pro-Life" advocacy, and his defense of his daughter's sexual orientation and recent abortion. "She is a valued member of our family," Stoppit explained.

Lesson 17

Walter Conrad • WPLA Evening News

Report on Subversives

CD track 17   Radio script page 107

TODAY'S RADIO NEWS

Relationship Prefixes: *super-, sur-, sub-, para-, epi-, hyper-, hypo-*

The prefixes in this lesson express the idea of a relationship. They modify the base to show that the new word is either "beyond" or "more than" the base or "beneath" or "less than" the base. For example:

> **superscript** – written above, such as πr^2
> **subscript** – written below, such as H_2O

The "super" prefixes are:

> ***super-*** = above, over, extra, additional
> ***sur-*** = above, over, additional
> ***epi-*** = above, over, around, outer
> ***hyper-*** = above, over, excessive
> ***para-*** = beyond, beside, near, outside

The "sub" prefixes are:

> ***sub-*** = under, beneath, less than
> ***hypo-*** = below, beneath

With some words the ***b*** in ***sub-*** changes to the first consonant of the base, or it is dropped. For example:

succumb	**supply**
suffix	**surrender**
suggest	**suspect**

Answers for Lesson 17 on page 86

Exercises

A . Use the prefix *super-* with one of the bases below to fill in the blanks in the sentence below.

-natural	-sonic	-fluous	-visor	-stitious
-sede	-man	-impose	-ficial	-star

1. That plane flies faster than sound. It is _____.
2. My boss is my _____.
3. My favorite comic book character is _____.
4. Bruce Springsteen is a _____.
5. Ghosts are _____ beings.
6. She doesn't like the number 13. She is _____.
7. The injuries are not deep or dangerous. They are _____.
8. To position one thing on top of another means to _____ one on the other.
9. His remarks were not necessary. They were _____.
10. These new regulations replace the old ones; they _____ the old ones.

B. Give the meaning of the underlined words in the following sentences.

1. She was appointed to an important subcommittee.

2. The Trident missile can be launched from a submerged submarine.

3. Let's take the subway; it's faster than the bus.

4. The government will support the farmers with a price subsidy.

5. The flood waters finally subsided and the citizens returned home.

6. After the countries suspended peace talks, the negotiator submitted a new proposal.

7. Do you subscribe to any magazines?

8. These plants grow in a subtropical climate.

9. They live outside the city in the suburbs.

10. The Central Bank should reduce the money supply.

11. Accept no substitute. Buy the real thing!

12. He was suspected of subversive activity against the government.

C. Use a *sur-* prefix with these bases in the following sentences.

-name	-passed	-charge	-prise	-face
-tax	-plus	-vivors	-vey	

1. There is a 3% _____.

2. There were no _____. Everybody died.

3. What a _____ , I didn't expect to see you here.

4. Please write your _____ on this line.

5. Is there a _____ for service on this bill?

6. The plane was hit by a _____-to-air missile.

7. The wheat crop has _____ our expectations. We will have a huge _____.

8. In a recent _____, the government found that 98% of all households have a TV.

D. Match the following words and phrases.

1. _____ epicenter   a. to restate something

2. _____ episode   b. an apparent contradiction

3. _____ hyperactive   c. one who says one thing, but does another

4. _____ hypothesis   d. always separated by the same distance

5. _____ hypocrite   e. an assumption

6. _____ paradox   f. like a chapter in a story

7. _____ paragraph   g. a fixed limit

8. _____ parallel   h. above the origin of an earthquake

9. _____ parameter   i. a division in writing

10. _____ paraphrase   j. overly active

E. Read the following story for general comprehension. Then highlight all the words with relationship prefixes.

Subcommittee Reports on Subversive Activity

HOLM, Nordia (PLN) The Subcommittee on un-Nordic Activity today published its annual survey of subversive activity. The subcommittee's findings came as no surprise to most observers. Among the conclusions and recommendations were:

• A plan has been submitted to the Interior Ministry to establish a permanent bureau to coordinate and supervise the surveillance of all suspected subversive activity. All government agencies now involved in the investigation of subversive activity would be subordinated to the proposed Superbureau of Investigation (SBI).

• Support for the clandestine International Anarchist Union has subsided in the state of Novgorovia. The state security office has also announced the formation of a new paramilitary unit to aid in the suppression of IAU terrorism. The unit will be equipped with automatic rifles and submachine guns.

• The mystery surrounding the September bombing of the Novgorovian hydroelectric substation has finally been dispelled. According to the subcommittee, the substation was not bombed, as originally supposed, by the IAU, but was destroyed by an angry employee who had been fired for insubordination.

• Superspy Dr. Oui, who surrendered to agent James Stock on the subtropical island of Epicuria, did not pass on significant secrets to Sudistan. However, Oui's accomplice Kitty Hawk, who is now suspected of supplying secret plans of the supersonic X-200 fighter, still has not surfaced.

SUPERSPY Dr. Oui and Kitty Hawk   *INTERPOL FILE XX*

• Detective supervisor Gridlock Homes, who survived an assassination attempt in a suburban subway station with only superficial wounds, has identified his assailant as a member of the Nordic underground. Apparently the attacker escaped in one of Nordurbia's many subterranean passageways.

Lesson 18

Movement Prefixes: *ex-, in-/im-, ad-, ab-, trans-, pro-*

This group of prefixes usually carries a meaning of movement in some direction: "out of," "into," "away from," "across," and "in front of."

ex- means "out of" or "from." For example:
   to export – to carry (or send) out of a country.

In some cases the prefix is only *e-*.
   erupt – to break out

   • *Note:* there is also another *ex-* prefix which always has a hyphen and means "former" or "previous": **ex-president** – former president

in- is also spelled *im-* when it is attached to a word that begins with *b, m,* or *p.*
It means "in," "into," or "within."
   income – (money) that comes in
   import – to carry (or bring) into a country

ad- and *ab-* have opposite meanings. *ad-* means "toward" or "to." *ab-* means "away from" or "from."
   administer – to serve to
   abduct – to lead from
The prefix *ad-* is often spelled with just the *a-,* and the first consonant of the base is doubled:
   a + fix = affix   **a + cept** = accept   **a + tain** = attain

trans- means "across."
   transportation – carrying something across (from one place to another)

pro- means "in front of" or "forward."
   to proceed – to move forward (*ceed* or *cede* is from Latin, and means "move.")

   • *Note:* there is also a *pro-* prefix that is usually hyphenated and means "for" or "in support of" For example: **pro-life** – in support of life. (This phrase is often used for the position of those who are against abortion.)

Answers for Lesson 18 on page 86

Exercises

A. Use the words in the list below and match them with a definition.

explode   expatriate   expand
income   immigrate   investigate
input   inhabitant   export
informant

1. _____ to become larger
2. _____ to move into a new country
3. _____ a person who lives outside his native country
4. _____ A bomb does this.
5. _____ to study something
6. _____ to send goods out of a country
7. _____ money that a person earns
8. _____ to enter information into a computer
9. _____ a person who lives in a place
10. _____ a person who gives information

B. Try to analyze and define the underlined words. If analysis doesn't help, study the context.

1. The abductors are holding a hostage.

   _____

2. He was an advisor to the president.

   _____

3. We will have to absorb the loss.

   _____

4. They continue to adhere to the policy of non-violence.

   _____

5. The weather has been abnormal.

   _____

6. The *-ly* suffix usually indicates an adverb.

   _____

7. In that country abortion is illegal.

   _____

8. Who will administer the test?

   _____

9. Adapting to a new culture is not always easy.

   _____

C. Use each of the words below in one of the sentences.

transitive   transcontinental   transplant
transfer   transmitter   transportation
translate   transactions

1. Can you _____ this into German?

2. This radio _____ is very powerful. It can send signals thousands of kilometers.

3. Which form of _____ will you take, bus or train?

4. He took a _____ flight from Senegal to Somalia.

5. This is a _____ verb; it requires an object.

6. The surgeons performed a successful heart _____ and the patient is doing well.

7. She made three _____ at her bank today.

8. I want to _____ from this department to another.

D. Match the following words with an appropriate phrase.

1. _____ proceed   a. the act of making something

2. _____ proposal   b. to act or speak against something

3. _____ prosecute   c. to continue

4. _____ propeller   d. an idea to be discussed or considered

5. _____ progress   e. to make something continue in time

6. _____ production   f. one who supports or speaks for something

7. _____ progressive   g. to bring action against someone in a court of law

8. _____ protest   h. forward-looking

9. _____ proponent   i. something that moves an airplane

10. _____ prolong   j. positive development, moving forward

E. Read the following article and then highlight all the words with prefixes of movement.

Exports Exceed Imports

Newly launched transoceanic cargo carrier NewlandiaStar *in Seal Bay last Friday*

PORTHAVEN, Newlandia (PLN) The Ministry of Finance and Trade yesterday announced that for the first quarter of the year, the total value of exports has exceeded imports for the first time since 1996.

The shift is due mostly to a significant increase in textile and electronic exports. According to a ministry spokesperson, "our intensive, three-year expansion of the textile industry has finally paid off. In fact, our textile production is even ahead of the projections we made when we initiated the project. So far, all indications are that the prospects for the remainder of the year are excellent."

The government also claimed that the investment in the development of the electronics sector has paid off and that income from the sales of electronics equipment is also beyond all expectations.

The maritime transportation project, however, has not progressed according to plan. Admitting that the government shipbuilding yards have fallen behind schedule, the Minister of Transportation blamed part of the reduced productivity at the Porthaven Shipyard on the prolonged shipfitters' strike last fall. The Minister has promised a full-scale investigation of the slow pace of construction of transoceanic cargo carriers.

First quarter imports were only slightly ahead of last year's first quarter. The administration claimed that its intensive "Buy Domestic" campaign is a major reason for the slow growth of imported goods. "Our automotive industry is making a successful transition from the production of full-scale models to economy cars, and the consumer reaction has been positive." "The Toyota invasion is over," asserted a government spokesperson.

The Ministry of Tourism also announced that the influx of tourists from Western Transfluvia has injected a considerable amount of foreign exchange into the economy.

"All in all," according to the Director of the Central Bank, "we are looking forward to a protracted period of economic progress, and although consumer prices rose somewhat in the first quarter, we are slowly winning the war against inflation and the budget deficit."

Lesson 19

Cindy Speakwell • WPLA Newsbreak
Students to Chancellor: Resign!
CD track 19   Radio script page 109

TODAY'S
RADIO NEWS

Movement Prefixes: *de-, re-, se-*

Although these prefixes generally suggest some kind of movement, their exact meanings are not always easy to see.

de- in Latin has a meaning of "from." But as an English prefix it can also mean "down," "away from," "the opposite of," or "undo" (the base). Look at this list of words to get a general understanding of the meaning of *de-*:

down	*away from*	*opposite/undo*
decrease	detain	deforestation
descend	deflect	deregulate
deflate	defend	depopulate

- *Note:* A hyphen may separate *de-* from its base when the base begins with *e*. For example, **de-escalate**.

re- in Latin means "back" or "again." Study these words in order to get an understanding of *re-*:

back	*again*
retain	reforestation
reject	reissue
return	reconfirm
reclaim	rebuild

- *Note:* As with *de-*, a hyphen may be used to separate *re-* from its base when the base begins with *e*. For example, **re-elect**.

se- has a general meaning of "aside," "by itself," or "apart from." The meaning of *se-* is not easy to see, and it is not hyphenated.

seclude	separate
select	seduce

Exercises

A.   Add either **de-** or **re-** to each of these bases to make a meaningful word.

   1. A _____odorant is used to counteract unpleasant smells.
   2. "I shall _____turn," said General MacArthur as he left the Philippines.
   3. The physicist Nils Groenig _____ceived an award for his _____search.
   4. The opposite of attach is _____tach.
   5. It is not a genuine piece of art; it is a _____production.
   6. The terrorists' objective is to _____stabilize the government.
   7. We were not told the truth; we were _____ceived.
   8. The government has just _____leased new information on the
       disastrous _____forestation of the tropical rain forests.

B.   Choose the best word for the sentence.

   1. As the flood waters began to (secede/recede) the people returned to their houses.

   2. That man has a very high opinion of himself, in other words, his ego is (deflated/inflated).

   3. The hot-air balloon crashed when it (deflated/inflated).

   4. The doctors tried everything but the patient's condition continued to (decline/recline).

   5. The Lazy-Boy chair is for relaxing or lying back. It is also called a (recliner/decliner) chair.

   6. (Segregation/Congregation) is a form of discrimination because it means to isolate or

       separate one group from another.

   7. The president was (selected/re-elected) for a second term of office.

   8. Several illegal immigrants were (detained/retained) by the Border Patrol.

C. Match the words below and the definitions:

1. cut off the head = _____

2. place authority in local hands = _____

3. cut back or cut down = _____

4. make something turn aside or away = _____

5. deteriorate or decay; lose value = _____

6. get off an airplane = _____

7. summarize, restate = _____

8. throw or bend back from a surface, like a mirror = _____

9. grow again = _____

10. bring back to life = _____

11. cause to think again or remember = _____

a. reflect	**d. recapitulate**	**g. revive**	**j decrease**
b. decapitate	**e. decentralize**	**h. deplane**	**k. degenerate**
c. deflect	**f. regenerate**	**i. remind**	

D. Use each of the following words only once to fill in the blanks in the following sentences:

reflect	**recapitulated**	**revive**	**decreased**
decapitated	**decentralize**	**deplane**	**degeneration**
deflected	**regenerate**	**reminded**	

1. Please stay in your seats with your seat belts fastened until we reach the airport terminal and the captain gives the signal for us to _____.

2. This octopus has only seven legs because one was cut off, but since it is able to _____, it will soon grow another leg.

3. The rescue team pulled the man from the water and tried to _____ him by administering mouth-to-mouth resuscitation.

4. In the French Revolution many people were _____. Not only the king and queen lost their heads.

5. The statement you have just heard does not _____ the view of the management.

6. In his speech he _____ the nation that the road to progress was difficult.

7. The village was saved because a rocky hill just above it _____ the landslide.

8. _____ or loss of muscle control is a feature of Parkinson's disease.

9. The chairman of the committee _____ the points discussed and then called for a vote.

10. France realized that it was necessary to _____ its banking procedures, as it was too time-consuming for all transactions to flow through the central bank in Paris.

11. A decompression chamber is used for divers whose bodies need to have pressure _____ slowly.

E. Read the following article for general comprehension. Then highlight the **de-**, **re-**, and **se-** prefixes.

Students Demand Chancellor's Resignation

Embattled NUE Chancellor   Photo: *Jerald News International*

ESTLANIA, Xenostan (PLN) Students at the National University in Estlania gathered outside the administration building Friday afternoon and chanted "Retire or rehire," directing their demands at the university chancellor. The chancellor recently dismissed half of the English faculty in the foreign language department on the grounds that the expatriate English instructors were from degenerate societies and consequently their potentially destructive influence could destabilize Estlanian society.

The chancellor declared that English would continue to be taught, but that the instructors would be replaced by local staff. The courses are to be restructured with emphasis on grammar and a substantial reduction in cultural content.

The decisions are part of the government's efforts to detach itself from the West. Recognizing that it cannot totally divorce itself from the West, however, the government announced that only fields related to national finance and security would remain untouched. A special group of students will be selected to continue studies in language and subjects related to business, finance, and defense. These students will be employed by the government for whatever projects require contact or advanced knowledge or technology from the West.

The protesting students, from the group Students for Free Expression, want the chancellor deposed, instructors reinstated, and the library restocked with the books and other materials that have been removed. The student association has talked of bringing suit against the government for withholding information and reducing the quality of Estlanian education. When asked about the charges, a government spokesman declined to comment.

For the past two days the chancellor has remained in seclusion in his living quarters, and has been unavailable for comment.

Lesson 20

Walter Conrad • WPLA Evening News
Union Sympathizers Walk

CD track 20   Radio script page 110

TODAY'S RADIO NEWS

"With" and "Against" Prefixes: *syn-, co-, contra-*

The prefixes in this lesson modify the meaning of the base by adding a meaning of either "togetherness" or "opposition to" the base meaning.

syn- is also spelled *sym-* before *h, m,* or *p*. It means "sharing with" or "together."
>   **sympathy** – feeling with or for (someone)

co-, which generally means "together," "with," or "equally," has several variant spellings: *con-, col-, com-,* and *cor-*. It is joined to a long list of Latin bases, and in many cases the "together" meaning is not easy to see. Therefore, analysis is not always helpful for understanding *co-* words.
>   **cooperate** – work together
>   **collapse** – fall together
>   **conduct** – lead together/with
>   **compress** – push together
>   **correspond** – answer back (and forth) together

contra- (also see Lesson 7 & 16) and a closely related form *counter-* have a meaning of "against" or "opposite."
>   **contradict** – say the opposite
>   **counteract** – act against

There is also a prefix *ob-*, with variant spellings *op-*, and *of-*, which can have a meaning of "against" or "facing," as in **opposite**, "to be positioned against." Others are:
>   **object**   **obstruct**   **obscure**   **oppress**   **offend**

Exercises

A. In column 2 are some "syn" words. Use them to fill in the blanks in column 1 to create common phrases.

	1		2
1.	a _____ shape	symbol
2.	_____ and analysis	sympathetic
3.	a _____ person	symphony
4.	a _____ orchestra	symmetrical
5.	_____ and antonym	symptoms
6.	a religious _____	synchronized
7.	_____ of a disease	synonym
8.	_____ movements	synthesis

B. In these sentences try to explain the meaning of *contra-* and *counter-* words. If analysis of the word does not help you, study the context.

1. Turn the dial in a counterclockwise direction.
   Counterclockwise _____
   _____

2. Contraception techniques are taught in birth-control clinics.
   Contraception _____
   _____

3. There are many counterfeit $100 bills in circulation.
   Counterfeit _____
   _____

4. We need to agree on this, so please don't contradict me.
   Contradict _____
   _____

5. This traveler's check has not been countersigned.
   Countersigned _____
   _____

6. In some places birth control is a very controversial subject.
   Controversial_____
   _____

7. After the initial battle, the defenders counterattacked.
   Counterattack _____
   _____

8. The negotiator refused to continue the dialogue with his counterpart.
   Counterpart _____
   _____

9. The identity of our counterspy cannot be revealed. It must remain secret.
   Counterspy _____
   _____

10. Some people called the hippie movement of the 60's a countercultural revolution.
    Countercultural _____
    _____

C. *com-* is prefixed to bases that begin with **b, m,** or **p.** Can you guess what *con-, col-,* and *cor-* are prefixed to? Add a prefix to these bases.

_____bine	_____pare	_____struct
_____cept	_____pose	_____relation
_____rect	_____serve	_____fident
_____lect	_____lateral	_____lide
_____form	_____mercial	_____trol
_____vict	_____nect	_____junction

D. *con-* is a common prefix. Here are some sentences from previous readings. Can you explain the *con-* words? These words are not always easy to analyze, so study the context.

1. The detainees were under investigation for criminal <u>conspiracy</u>.
2. The list of arrests may grow as the investigation <u>continues</u>.
3. A spokesman has <u>confirmed</u> that the airliner was carrying tourists.
4. They will begin a search for the wreckage when weather <u>conditions</u> permit.
5. The novel was acclaimed as a major <u>contribution</u> to world literature.
6. He is the resident <u>conductor</u> at the Thyme <u>conservatory</u> of music.
7. Robert Rackham is a well-known forestry <u>consultant</u>.
8. He claimed the <u>Conservative</u> Union Party was apathetic.
9. He <u>concluded</u> by saying that his party would be victorious again.
10. He covered up his <u>conviction</u> in 1981 for embezzling funds from the First Andean Bank.
11. <u>Condolences</u> poured into the capital of Territoria as the citizens began a three-day mourning period for the death of R. J. Lee.
12. Mainland coastal areas <u>contain</u> nearly one-third of the world's population.
13. They met to set the agenda for the forthcoming disarmament <u>conference</u>.
14. The minister promised an investigation of the slow pace of <u>construction</u> of transoceanic cargo carriers.
15. <u>Consumer</u> prices rose somewhat in the first quarter.

E. Choose the best word for each of these sentences.

object	**obscured**	**obverse**	**oppose**	**offensive**
obstruct	**opponents**	**objection**	**offend**	

1. If you don't _____, I will leave now.
2. Please don't _____ the path. Keep it clear.
3. I found his jokes to be very _____, crude and tasteless.
4. The two _____ played a great game until finally the Wildcats won.
5. It's on the _____ side. Turn it over and look.
6. The clouds _____ our view of the moon.
7. I hope I didn't _____ you when I said you were overweight.
8. I won't _____ your decision to drop out of college, but it's a bad one.
9. The judge overruled the lawyer's _____ to the prosecutor's question.

F. Read the following passage for general comprehension. Then go through it again, highlighting all the words with **syn-**, **con-**, **ob-**, and **contra-** prefixes.

Union Sympathizers Walk off the Job

Concordia, NA (PLN) Yesterday morning over 350 Transcontinental Airways pilots and flight attendants refused to cross picket lines of the striking Ground Crew Union, leaving thousands of passengers stranded. Airports throughout the eastern part of the country were congested with angry commuters and travelers. Incoming passengers at Concordia Airport were forced to seek ground connections to the many regional cities serviced by TCA.

Meanwhile, union negotiators, meeting with TCA officials, are opposed to a compromise solution. TCA had offered a 10% salary increase in response to the union's demands for a 15% pay hike. The collapse of the talks came after seven consecutive days of collective bargaining. At the heart of the contract dispute is the union's insistence that their salaries have not kept pace with inflation. "Our salaries have remained constant for two years now, while inflation continues to constrict the purchasing power of our income. Ten percent isn't enough," objected one angry baggage handler.

At a press conference late yesterday afternoon, an airline spokesman said, "We want to cooperate with the union. Coexistence is our goal, but according to our consultants, our offer to the union matches what our competitors are paying. We made a sincere offer to the negotiators, hoping to avoid

Pilots and flight attendants support GCU.   MJP

this confrontation, but our counterparts have simply chosen to obstruct negotiations."

Contacted at his Contracoastal beach condominium, Meriwether P. Barnstormer, principal owner of TCA, issued a brief comment on the crisis: "I am confident we will find a satisfactory conclusion to this confusion. TCA however, will not be coerced into signing a contract that would compel us to increase airfares, and I am convinced that the union's demands would force us to do just that."

Asked if the pilots' walkout was simply a one-day gesture, striking pilot Harlan Wing insisted that the pilots were 100% behind the Ground Crew Union. According to Wing, the conflict is actually a symptom of some very serious differences between Barnstormer and the airline he controls.

Lesson 21

Maria Ventura • WPLA The Morning Show
Pandemic Inevitable

CD track 21

Radio script page 111

TODAY'S RADIO NEWS

Greek Bases and Affixes

During the Renaissance period (1500-1650) there was a great interest in England in Greek and Latin. One important impact and result of this interest is that English acquired many new words, especially in the fields of science, technology, and health. Even today we continue to borrow from Greek to name new medicines or procedures, such as *laparoscope* or *laparoscopy* and *astronaut*, from *astros* meaning star/outer space and *nautes* meaning sailor.

Many bases and affixes refer to the physical aspect of our world.

> *phys-* – nature
> *astro-* – star or outer space
> *atmos-* – vapor/gas
> *geo-* – earth or earthlike
> *bio-* – life
> *zoo-* – animal or animal kingdom
> *phon-* – sound
> *spher-* – ball
> *cycl-* – circle

Some of these words can combine with each other.

> **atmosphere**
> **biosphere**

hemi- means half, and so **hemisphere** would be half a ball.

These bases refer to human life, parts of the body, or its condition:
> *dem-* – people
> *anthropo-* – human beings
> *psych-* – mind
> *path-* – disease
> *gen-* – origins, family, source
> *geronto/geront-* – old age
> *ophthalmo/ophthalm-* – eye, eyeball

The suffix *-ology* means study of (something), and the suffix *-ist* attached to *-olog(y)* means one who studies (something): **geologist**, **psychologist**, etc.

Answers for Lesson 21 on page 87

Exercises

A1. Complete the definition of these combinations:

Hemisphere – _____ of the earth

Biosphere – the part of the earth that can support _____

Atmosphere – the mass of _____ around the earth

A2. Combine a base from page 75 with *-ology* to produce a word that means the study of (something).

the earth: _____

the stars: _____

living things: _____

aging/old age: _____

diseases: _____

the mind: _____

sounds: _____

human beings: _____

A3. Can you make some more *-ology* words?

_____   _____   _____

_____   _____   _____

A4. A person who studies zoology is a zoologist. What do these people do?

biologist _____

geologist _____

astrologist _____

zoologist _____

psychologist _____

ophthalmologist _____

gerontologist _____

pathologist _____

A5. These words can take an *-ic* or an *-ic + -al* adjective ending. Add an ending. What do they mean?

spher_____   _____

zoolog_____   _____

astrolog_____   _____

biolog_____   _____

psycholog_____   _____

atmospher_____   _____

phonolog_____   _____

patholog_____   _____

Many bases and words in the medical field come from Greek.

pharma- – drug

-scope – see

arthr(o)- – joint

dermat- – skin

gastr(o)- – stomach

hepat(o)- – liver

laryng(o)- – throat, where the voice box is

B. The suffix *-itis* means inflammation or disease of. Complete the sentences below with an appropriate combination of a base **+** *-itis*. Use the bases above.

1. People who played a lot of sports often suffer from _____ or aching and swelling in their joints when they get older.

2. _____ is an irritation or inflammation of the skin.

3. Fred can't talk because he has _____ .

4. My sister had _____, so she avoids alcohol and heavy foods that affect the liver.

5. Bob suffers from _____ and therefore doesn't eat spicy or hot foods, which irritate his stomach.

In addition to being used in the fields of science and health, Greek bases also form the basis for many words that pertain to psychological and social aspects of humanity.

dem- – people

-phobia – fear

phil- – love

-soph- – wisdom, knowledge

-gnos- – knowing

-logo – word, speech

-archy/ -cracy – govern/rule

C. Look these words up and look for their Greek bases.

homophobia	**democracy**	**philosophy**	**endemic**
photography	**agnostic**	**theology**	**anarchy**

D. Read the following passage for general comprehension. Then go through it again, highlighting all the words that have Greek bases.

World Health Officials Warn: Pandemic Inevitable

GENERA (PLN) At a press conference this morning in Genera, world health officials from both hemispheres warned that it is just a matter of time before a pandemic of disastrous and catastrophic proportions strikes. The director of World Health Watch, Ashok Lalwani, gave examples of pandemics in history, explained the conditions required for a pandemic, listed possible future scenarios, and then outlined steps to minimize a pandemic.

Well-known disastrous pandemics from the past include typhoid fever, the bubonic plague, smallpox, and cholera. The domestication of animals has resulted in pandemics called zoonoses – diseases that can be transmitted from animals to humans. Examples include rabies, influenza, tuberculosis, and Asian Bird Flu, possibly the next pandemic.

To be declared a pandemic, a disease must meet three conditions. It must:

- not be endemic to the population or the geographical area
- infect humans with a serious illness
- spread quickly and sustainably from human to human

To build to pandemic level, diseases progress through a cycle starting with (1) Interpandemic (no diagnosed disease in humans, but a danger of animal-to-human transmission), (2) a pandemic alert (an epidemic infection in humans but still local, contained outbreaks), and finally (3) the pandemic (very widespread infection and sustainability of the disease, even on a worldwide basis).

Future Pandemics: Pathologists, epidemiologists, and biologists are keeping a watchful eye on Marburg virus and Ebola virus, as potential candidates for pandemics. Though lethal, for now they

Dr. Ashok Lalwani at Minneapolis seminar last May

are not able to spread quickly because transmission of the diseases requires close physical contact from one human to another. The concern is that the diseases could develop genetic mutations that will spread the disease more rapidly.

Lalwani emphasized the importance of developing an International Pandemic Plan. The plan must address communication – informing the public to avoid panic; implementation of non-pharmaceutical measures such as travel advisories and limited social interaction; containment of the disease to limit the spread; identification of the source to prevent further infection; development of antiviral vaccines and other measures; and educating the public about good health practices.

Lesson 22

Review of Bases, Affixes, and Compounds

First read the editorial; then make a list of at least twenty bases and affixes plus at least five compounds.

Editorial:
Poverty, Terror, and Climate Change

Today the U.N. announced the formation of a new agency whose mission will be to counter the disastrous impact of climate change as it relates to poverty and terrorism. Prior to the establishment of the new agency, a select committee of international scientists and political and military leaders released the results of a two-year investigation. The statement below summarizes the committee's findings.

Although religious fundamentalism has long been associated with terrorism, the committee focused on the connection between climate change and terrorism. In the past few decades, one obvious result of climate change has been the expansion of uninhabitable desert and barely habitable semi-desert land and the reduction of productive land areas. At the same time, population growth continues to put pressure on inhabitable land. The result is more people trying to live off less and less land. Per-capita productivity is reduced and the people in affected areas become poorer. Conflict over available land increases along ethnic lines. At least part of the terrible genocide in Darfur has been attributed to this phenomenon.

In many areas, so-called progress and economic development lead to environmental degradation. Important forests are cut. This in turn contributes to climate change, even on a worldwide basis. The destruction of the Amazon rainforest is the classic example in this twenty-first century.

The vicious cycle of climate change and increasing poverty often leads to violence. And much of the violence is in the form of terrorism, sometimes as thinly disguised government policy. Certainly, religious, racial, national, and ethnic tensions are some of the root causes of terrorism, but these factors are often exacerbated by the increase in poverty.

The danger is not limited to marginal areas such as Saharan Africa. Consider the effect of rising sea levels. First low-lying islands are inundated. The inhabitants flee to other, higher islands and mainlands. Conflicts develop. Then, large urban centers are under water. Major population shifts occur. The picture is not pretty, even in developed countries.

The time has come for international cooperation and action. The time has come for sane national policy on over-consumption of natural resources and industrial pollution driven by the need to acquire and the simple act of throwing away. The time has come for every reader of this paper and every citizen of this town to take action, even if it is only buying long-life light bulbs.

List at least twenty bases and affixes plus at least five compounds.

Bases	**Affixes**	**Compounds**

Answers

Lesson 1 *page 3*

• *NOTE: Words repeated in the news article are given only once in the answer key.*

Uncover<u>ed</u> • sa<u>id</u>• detain<u>ed</u> • suspect<u>ed</u> terrorist<u>s</u> • discover<u>ed</u> • explosive<u>s</u> hidd<u>en</u> • weapon<u>s</u> • tak<u>en</u> • rai<u>ded</u> locations • prevent<u>ed</u> • prosecutor<u>'s</u> detainee<u>s</u> • source<u>s</u> • be<u>en</u> • plann<u>ing</u> carri<u>ed</u> • unnam<u>ed</u> • neighbo<u>ring</u> officer<u>s</u> • discover<u>ed</u> • warrant<u>s</u> • issu<u>ed</u> ringleader<u>s</u> • agent<u>s</u> • investigation<u>s</u> handl<u>ing</u> • agency<u>'s</u> • large<u>st</u> • expect<u>ed</u> arrest<u>s</u> • long<u>er</u> • continue<u>s</u>

Lesson 2 *page 5*

Exercise A
1. one who speaks for another
2. a leader, especially of an illegal group
3. secret
4. a collection, a forced gathering
5. a place where goods are stored

Exercise B
1. failure of the heart
2. a conservative political group
3. seven people who belong to a group
4. a stop to war
5. a period of five years
6. at an important position
7. supported by the government
8. having no smoke, exempt from import tax
9. two identical engines

Exercise E
Airliner • Aircraft • outbound • turbojet state-owned • airline • NATIONAIR fighter-bomber • takeoff • Gulfside Airport • hour-long • eyewitnesses midair • twin-engine • jetliner thunderstorm • daybreak • spokeswoman seaside • Air-sea • rainstorm shark-infested • life jackets • air-miles mainland • frogmen • underwater

Lesson 3 *page 8*

Exercise A1
1. f, 2. d, 3. e, 4. a, 5. b, 6.c

Exercise A2
1. conductor: carrier
2. graduate: to go in a series of steps (leave school)
3. recede: move back or down
4. export: to carry out (trade)
5. promote: to move forward (in a career)
6. mission: something sent somewhere

Exercise B1
1. c, 2. a, 3. d, 4. h, 5. g, 6. e, 7. b, 8. f

Exercise B2
1. conclusion: end
2. receipt: proof of getting
3. reject: to throw back (or away)
4. subtract: to pull down (reduce)
5. retain: to hold (back)
6. accident: happening
7. activist: one who takes action

Exercise C1
1. e, 2. g, 3. a, 4. d, 5. c,
6. f, 7. b, 8. h, 9. i

Exercise C2
1. incredible: unbelievable
2. tense: tight, nervous
3. claimed: stated, said
4. regulations: rules, laws
5. dictator: one who says what to do
6. mediator: one who comes between
7. inscription: something written in or on
8. pose: sit, take a position
9. instructions: information, directions

Exercise D
<u>claim</u>ed • <u>conduct</u>ing • <u>media</u> • in<u>cred</u>ibly <u>act</u>ion • <u>pred</u>icted • re<u>act</u>ed • pro<u>pos</u>ing ob<u>ject</u>ed • <u>claim</u>ing • dis<u>rupt</u> • ex<u>tract</u>ing transp<u>ort</u>ing • dis<u>rupt</u>ive • transp<u>ort</u>ed • <u>Port</u> ex<u>ceed</u>ingly • <u>Motor</u> • in<u>ject</u> • ex<u>pos</u>ing <u>tens</u>ion • <u>intens</u>ive • con<u>clud</u>ed <u>construct</u>ing • de<u>struct</u>ion • <u>correct</u>ed in<u>cred</u>ible • con<u>tain</u>ed • in<u>clud</u>ing • <u>activ</u>ity <u>gradu</u>ally • de<u>scrib</u>ed • su<u>cces</u>s

Lesson 4 *page 13*

Exercise A
reporter	marcher
creditor	kidnapper
writer	director
professor	designer
buyer	trader
leader	voter
manager	rioter
employer	lawyer
prosecutor	foreigner
worker	survivor
flier	dealer
prisoner	photographer
planner	demonstrator
commander	advisor
inspector	supporter
exporter	governor
farmer	murderer
hijacker	forecaster
liar	actor
traveler	interpreter
investigator	officer
negotiator	defector

Exercise B
1. passenger	7. traitor
2. doctor	8. chancellor
3. member	9. minister
4. soldier	10. neighbor
5. ambassador	11. victor
6. mayor	

Exercise C
1. i, 2. c, 3. g, 4. h, 5. d, 6. a,
7. k, 8. f, 9. j, 10. e, 11. b

Exercise D
1. employee, employer
2. detainee
3. trainer, trainee
4. payer, payee
5. addressee

Exercise E
1. profiteer	4. auctioneer
2. pamphleteer	5. volunteer
3. racketeer	6. engineer

Exercise F
• negotiator • kidnappers • ambassador
• reporters • captors • members • prisoners
• adviser • interpreter • leader • foreigners
• workers • travelers • mayor • councilors
• demonstrators • marchers • supporters
• commander • investigator

Lesson 5 *page 17*

Exercise A
1. scientist
2. sociologists, psychologists, psychiatrists
3. economist, capitalists, socialists, communists
4. dramatist, novelist, columnist
5. guitarist, violinist, pianist, cellist, flutist
6. realists, idealists
7. activist, anarchist, environmentalist, ecologist
8. arsonist, terrorist, rapist
9. tourist, motorist

Exercise B

1. b, 2. e, 3. a, 4. f, 5. c, 6. d

Exercise C
1. migrant
2. opponent
3. consultant
4. accountant
5. occupant
6. patient
7. immigrant
8. dissident
9. resident

Exercise D
1. armory
2. bakery
3. dictionary
4. directory
5. diary
6. laboratory
7. library
8. treasury
9. factory
10. territory
11. mortuary
12. chemistry

Exercise F
One who: Artists • Scientists • winners
panelist • Physicist • assistants • botanist
professor • chemist • novelist • dramatist
Antillian • recipient • Idealist • author
dissident • resident • composer • pianist
musicians • proponent • conductor
environmentalist • consultant • activist
Proletarian • Capitalist

Place where: laboratory • Diary
• Conservatory • forestry

Lesson 6 *page 21*

Exercise B
independent
immature
irresponsible
indefinite
imperfect
immoral
incapable
indirect
imbalance
insecure
illogical
irrational
insane
illiterate
improper

Exercise C
1. nonsmoker
2. non-Moslem
3. nonfiction
4. nonstop
5. nonviolence
6. nonsense
7. nontoxic
8. nonconformist
9. nonpayment
10. non-Arab
11. nonmember
12. nonperforming

Exercise D
Nonresident • Independent • illegally
uninterested • illegal • unattractive
unrewarding • unemployment • Unskilled
uneducated • illiterate • irresponsible
unlimited • non-Lowlanders • inadequate
unrest • unemployed

Lesson 7 *page 23*

Exercise A
1. antiaircraft: used against aircraft
2. antiabortion: opposing abortion
3. antipathy: opposite feeling
4. Anti-Semitism: against Semites (Jews)
5. antitrust: regulation against trusts
6. antonyms: opposite words or meanings

Exercise B
1. atypical
2. anarchy
3. apolitical
4. amoral
5. anesthetic
6. asexual
7. anonymous
8. amorphous
9. atheism
10. apathy
11. anaerobic
12. asymmetry

Exercise D
1. misbehave
2. misjudge
3. misfortune
4. malnutrition
5. misprint
6. malcontent
7. mismanage
8. malfunction
9. misguide
10. misplace
11. malpractice
12. misfit
13. mislead
14. maladjusted
15. misspell

Exercise E
Disagree • differentiated • diverse
apathetic • antipollution • mismanagement
unregulated • anarchy • malcontents
misfits • disruption • disturbance
Anti-Everything Party • misguided
maladjusted • atheists • misappropriated
malignant • misled • misinformed
dismissed • malpractice • malnutrition
divisive • amoral • unworthy
misgovernment • mistake • misplace
misfired

Lesson 8 *page 26*

Exercise A
1. two
2. three
3. one
4. one
5. two
6. same
7. trilingual
8. having many languages
9. all
10. monochromatic
11. tri
12. many, many
13. bilateral
14. uni
15. half of a colon
16. every six months or half a year
17. semiprivate
18. semicircle
19. multinational
20. equilateral

Exercise B
multimedia
bimonthly, semimonthly
multiskilled, semiskilled
multivitamin
semicircular
bifocal
semifinal
multimillionaire
multipurpose
multicultural, bicultural
semiprecious
bicentenary
equidistant

Exercise C
Polyglot: speaking many languages
bilingual: speaking two languages
bimonthly: twice a month or every two
   months
multilingual: many languages
monotony: one (boring) tone

Exercise D
Pan-Equatorian • semiannual
multimillion • tri-state • equidistant
monorail • unify • multitude
multilingual • trilingual • bilingual
Polytechnic • biennial • bilateral

Lesson 9 *page 30*

Exercise A
soften   widen   entrust   endorse
endanger enclose loosen   encourage
enable   engage   endure   encounter
deepen   brighten enforce enhance
employ   weaken   embrace engulf

Exercise B
1. betrayed
2. bewildering
3. bereaved, bemoaned
4. bedeviled
5. behooves
6. beware
7. belittle
8. besieged
9. beclouded

Exercise C
1. demonstrate
2. immigrate
3. nationalize
4. dramatized
5. assassinated
6. investigate
7. negotiated
8. graduate
9. operate
10. terrorized
11. legalized
12. speculate

Exercise D
1. identify
2. activate
3. locate
4. classify
5. falsify
6. unify
7. capitalize
8. equalize
9. tolerate
10. simplify
11. appropriate
12. differentiate
13. civilize
14. idealize
15. romanticize
16. intensify
17. finalize
18. certify

Exercise E
Intensifies • prosecution • strengthen
testify • operating • distributes
identified • terrorized • located
characterizing • centralize • distributors
immigrated • naturalized • falsified
naturalization • embezzling • employed
speculating • Bewildered • besieged
investigated • Enforcement • recognize
classified • betray • assassinate
frighten • prosecute

Lesson 10 *page 33*

Exercise A
1. intelligence
2. assurance
3. presidency
4. conspiracy
5. disturbance
6. candidacy
7. agency
8. disappearance
9. residence, residency
10. assistance
11. dissidence
12. democracy
13. insistence
14. preference
15. illiteracy
16. difference
17. conference
18. independence

Exercise B
1. similarity
2. humanity
3. familiarity
4. captivity
5. equality
6. Safety
7. activity
8. Security

Exercise C
1. steadiness
2. unworthiness
3. correctness
4. stillness
5. kindness
6. hopelessness
7. carelessness
8. helpfulness
9. foolishness
10. carefulness, business

Exercise D
1. citizenship
2. statehood
3. neighborhood
4. leadership
5. childhood
6. censorship
7. craftsmanship
8. dictatorship
9. Brotherhood
10. statesmanship

Exercise E
Independence • Condolences • residence
neighborhood • Brotherhood • ownership
apprenticeship • experiences • Unity
disobedience • prominence • democracy
candidacy • Equality • Opportunity
nationhood • fairness • tolerance
minority • dictatorship • presidency
statesmanship • adherence • nonviolence
Conference

Lesson 11 page 37

Exercise A

1. investigate	15. pollute
2. locate	16. disrupt
3. prevent	17. reject
4. prosecute	18. indicate
5. collide	19. conclude
6. confirm	20. organize
7. identify	21. present
8. demonstrate	22. provide
9. acclaim	23. graduate
10. contribute	24. cooperate
11. immigrate	25. recognize
12. oppose	26. elect
13. erupt	27. operate
14. administer	28. explode

Exercise B

1. appointment	8. development
2. announcement	9. requirement
3. expect (x)	10. contribute (x)
4. management	11. compose (x)
5. government	12. establishment
6. statement	13. movement
7. criticize (x)	

Exercise C

conservatism (a conservative)
criticism (a critic)

Exercise D

1. wreckage
2. coverage
3. footage
4. stardom
5. sewage, sewerage
6. postage
7. freedom
8. package
9. carriage
10. spoilage
11. martyrdom
12. boredom
13. marriage
14. baggage
15. breakage
16. brokerage

Exercise E

Assassination • Investigation • government declaration • administration • Kingdom terrorism • identification • announcement Information • Freedom • faction Organization • Nationalism • martyrdom Department's • direction • television footage • speculation • carriage reception • explosion • package wreckage • statement • disruption continuation

Lesson 12 page 41

Exercise A

1. believable	10. responsible
2. permissible	11. tolerable
3. receivable	12. reasonable
4. questionable	13. predictable
5. advisable	14. defensible
6. possible	15. considerable
7. acceptable	16. credible
8. measurable	17. manageable
9. operable	18. defendable

Exercise B

1. recognizable
2. tolerable
3. odorless
   colorless
   detectable
4. likeable
5. enjoyable
6. collapsible
7. fruitless
8. flexible
9. hopeless
10. fashionable

Exercise C

1. wooden
2. suicidal
3. oral
4. optional
5. floral
6. oval
7. woolen, thermal
8. golden
9. formal
10. earthen

Exercise D

1. e, 2. i, 3. g, 4. a, 5. c,
6. h, 7. d, 8. j, 9. b, 10. f

Exercise E

Annual • wooden • enjoyable • incredible Nationals • final • golden • quarterfinals unhittable • unbelievable • winless flawless • unable • semi-finals • tropical unstoppable • hopeless • fearless tireless • effortless • hitless • reliable impossible • believable

Lesson 13 page 44

Exercise A

migratory birds: birds that move from one
   place to another
respiratory illness: a problem with breathing
purposeful activity: an activity with a
   purpose
dangerous weapon: a weapon that can be
   harmful
scandalous affair: a shameful matter
monotonous sound: a sound that does not
   change (boring)
helpful advise: useful information
skillful politician: a clever politician
snowy weather: a snowstorm
silky fabric: cloth that is like silk
starry sky: a sky full of stars

Exercise B

1. hopeful
2. cautious
3. revolutionary
4. culinary
5. careful
6. precautionary
7. infectious
8. greasy, starchy
9. foggy
10. luxurious

Exercise C

1. ridiculous	10. primary
2. oily	11. faithful
3. thankful	12. envious
4. scary	13. icy
5. greedy	14. melodious
6. ambitious	15. pearly
7. thoughtful	16. secondary
8. inflationary	17. purposeful
9. fictitious	18. visionary

Exercise D

1. snowy	6. dusty	11. rainy
2. windy	7. icy	12. smoggy
3. muddy	8. hazy	13. cloudy
4. chilly	9. smoky	14. misty
5. foggy	10. sunny	

Exercise E

Disastrous • mountainous • rocky temporary • voluntary • primary powerful • unwary • ordinary Regulatory • sturdy • hilly • Dangerous previous • rainy • sandy • Secondary Generous • thoughtful • parliamentary military

Lesson 14 *page 47*

Exercise A
1. heroic
2. schizophrenic
3. constructive
   destructive
4. brownish
5. boyish, comic
6. selfish
7. creative
8. foolish
9. acidic

Exercise B
1. metallic
2. sluggish
3. microscopic
4. conclusive
5. girlish, fortyish
6. geometric
7. organic
8. fantastic
9. brackish
10. collective

Exercise C
1. greenish/grayish
2. destructive
3. attractive
4. ticklish
5. scientific
6. italic
7. metric
8. corrective
9. basic

Exercise D

NOUN	VERB
magnet	magnetize
telephone	telephone
system	systematize
explosion	explode
creation, creativity	create
defense	defend
conclusion	conclude
disruption	disrupt
progression, progress	progress
decision	decide
production	produce

Exercise E
Turkish Swedish English Danish
Scottish Finnish Irish Spanish
British

Exercise F
•Dramatic • idyllic • massive • extensive
•frantic • heroic • sluggish • destructive
•feverish • classic • unselfish • decisive
•terrific

Lesson 15 *page 51*

Exercise A
1. federally
2. automatically
3. apparently
4. intelligently
5. normally
6. politically
7. ideally
8. environmentally
9. conservatively
10. illegally
11. financially
12. steadily
13. responsibly
14. nationally
15. appropriately
16. immediately
17. peacefully
18. successfully
19. cleverly
20. independently
21. democratically
22. fairly
23. progressively
24. securely

Exercise B
1. steadily
2. actively
3. fairly
4. securely
5. successfully
6. conservatively
7. normally
8. nationally
9. Apparently
10. environmentally
11. immediately
12. peacefully
13. illegally
14. automatically
15. appropriately

Exercise C
1. d, 2. g, 3. h, 4. a, 5. j,
6. i, 7. e, 8. b, 9. f, 10. c

Exercise D
1. downward
2. skyward
3. outward
4. lengthwise
5. backward
6. homeward
7. Otherwise
8. toward
9. forward
10. inward

Exercise E
Definitely • internationally • dramatically
invariably • steadily• globally • directly
absolutely • unquestionably • conclusively
indirectly • significantly • Accordingly
principally • sorely • certainly • politically
economically • densely • especially
partially • completely • severely • nearly
Additionally • drastically • increasingly
currently • immediately • forward
backward

Lesson 16 *page 55*

Exercise A
Pre

precaution	premature
preview	pre-Moslem
preschool	predict
prehistoric	prejudice
prepare	prevent
	prescription

Post
postpone
postgraduate
postscript

Pre and/or Post

pre-war	postwar
pre-trial	post-trial
prepay	postpay
prenatal	postnatal
precolonial	postcolonial

Exercise B
1. intermission
2. interview
3. international
4. interrupt
5. interpreter
6. intermediate
7. intersection
8. Intercollegiate
9. interstate

Exercise C
1. extracurricular: not part of the regular curriculum
2. intramural: internal; within the walls of the university
3. extragalactic: beyond our galaxy
4. extrovert: outgoing; interested in others
   introvert: inward-looking;
      interested in one's own thoughts
5. intravenously: within the veins
6. extraordinary: beyond the ordinary; unusual
7. introspection: self-examination
8. extrasensory: outside normal senses
9. contradict: say the opposite

Exercise D
intracoastal • International
intercontinental • postponed • prevent
pre-conference • interview • interfere
extraordinarily • posterity • precedes
contraceptives • post-demonstration
prepared • interrupt • interpreter
prelude • post-workshop • introduce
extravagant • contradictory

Lesson 17 *page 59*

Exercise A
1. supersonic
2. supervisor
3. Superman
4. superstar
5. supernatural
6. superstitious
7. superficial
8. superimpose
9. superfluous
10. supersede

Exercise B
1. subcommittee: division of a larger committee
2. submerged: went under water
   submarine: ship that operates under water
3. subway: a way underground; metro
4. support: help
   subsidy: price support
5. subsided: went down (receded)
6. suspended: stopped
   submitted: handed in
7. subscribe: sign up for/receive regularly
8. subtropical: zone between the tropical and temperate regions
9. suburbs: outside the city
10. supply: source
11. substitute: a replacement for something
12. suspected: thought to be
    subversive: working against

Exercise C
1. surtax
2. survivors
3. surprise
4. surname
5. surcharge
6. surface
7. surpassed
   surplus
8. survey

Exercise D
1. h, 2. f, 3. j, 4. e, 5. c,
6. b, 7. i, 8. d, 9. g, 10. a

Exercise E
Subcommittee • Subversive • survey
surprise • submitted • supervise
surveillance • suspected • subordinated
Super Bureau • Support • subsided
paramilitary • suppression • submachine
surrounding • substation • supposed
insubordination • Superspy • surrendered
subtropical • supplying • supersonic
surfaced • supervisor • survived
suburban • subway • superficial
subterranean

Lesson 18 *page 63*

Exercise A
1. expand
2. immigrate
3. expatriate
4. explode
5. investigate
6. export
7. income
8. input
9. inhabitant
10. informant

Exercise B
1. abductors: those who carry away; kidnappers
2. advisor: one who sees something; gives advice to
3. absorb: take up; accept
4. adhere to: stick to
5. abnormal: away from or not normal
6. adverb: modifies a verb (or adjective)
7. abortion: taking something away; especially an unborn baby
8. administer: conduct; give
9. adapting to: fitting into; adjusting to

Exercise C
1. translate
2. transmitter
3. transportation
4. transcontinental
5. transitive
6. transplant
7. transactions
8. transfer

Exercise D
1. c, 2. d, 3. g, 4. i, 5. j
6. a, 7. h, 8. b, 9. f, 10. e

Exercise E
Exports • Exceed • Imports • increase
intensive • expansion • industry
production • projections • initiated
project • indications • prospects
excellent • investment • income
expectations • transportation • progressed
productivity • prolonged • promised
investigation • transoceanic • imported
transition • invasion • asserted • influx
Transfluvia • injected • exchange
protracted • progress • inflation

Lesson 19 *page 67*

Exercise A
1. de, 2. re, 3. re, re, 4. de,
5. re, 6. de, 7. de, 8. re, de

Exercise B
1. recede
2. inflated
3. deflated
4. decline
5. reclining
6. Segregation
7. re-elected
8. detained

Exercise C
1. b, 2. e, 3. j, 4. c, 5. k, 6. h,
7. d, 8. a, 9. f, 10. g, 11. i

Exercise D
1. deplane
2. regenerate
3. revive
4. decapitated
5. reflect
6. reminded
7. deflected
8. Degeneration
9. recapitulated
10. decentralize
11. decreased

Exercise E
Demand • Resignation • Retire • rehire
department • degenerate • destructive
destabilize • declared • replaced
restructured • reduction • decisions
detach • Recognizing • related • remain
selected • defense • require • Expression
deposed • reinstated • restocked • removed
reducing • declined • remained • seclusion

Lesson 20 page 71

Exercise A
1. a symmetrical shape
2. synthesis and analysis
3. a sympathetic person
4. a symphony orchestra
5. synonym and antonym
6. a religious symbol
7. symptoms of a disease
8. synchronized movements

Exercise B
1. counterclockwise: against the normal progression of the clock, i.e. backwards
2. contraception: to prevent conception or the fertilization of an egg
3. counterfeit: illegally printed
4. contradict: say the opposite of
5. countersigned: a second, confirming signature
6. controversial: an issue having opposite points of view
7. counterattack: to return an attack
8. counterpart: someone who has a similar position
9. counterspy: a spy who tries to catch spies
10. countercultural: against the traditional culture

Exercise C

combine	compare	construct
concept	compose	correlation
correct	conserve	confident
collect	collateral	collide
conform	commercial	control
convict	connect	conjunction

Exercise D
1. conspiracy: to breathe together, i.e. an illegal plan or group
2. continues: to remain in existence
3. confirm: to state as true
4. condition: a state of being
5. contribution: something that is given
6. conductor: leader of a group (of musicians)
   conservatory: a music school
7. consultant: one who is consulted; one who supplies advice
8. conservative: a point of view that preserves the usual order; moderate, cautious
9. conclude: to bring to an end
10. conviction: to be found guilty
11. condolences: expressions of sorrow
12. contain: to enclose or include
13. conference: a meeting to discuss something
14. construction: the act of building
15. consumer: one who uses, like a customer

Exercise E
1. object
2. obstruct
3. offensive
4. opponents
5. obverse
6. obscured
7. offend
8. oppose
9. objection

Exercise F.
Sympathizers • congested • commuters
Concordia • connections • opposed
compromise • collapse • consecutive
collective • contract • constant • continues
constrict • objected • conference
cooperate • Coexistence • consultants
competitors • confrontation • counterparts
obstruct • Contacted • Contracoastal
condominium • comment • confident
conclusion • confusion • coerced • compel
convinced • conflict • symptom • controls

Lesson 21 page 75

Exercise A1
half of the earth
life
air

Exercise A2
geology
astrology
biology
gerontology
pathology
psychology
phonology
anthropology

Exercise A4
biologist: studies life
geologist: studies the earth
astrologist: studies stars in the Zodiac (note the difference from astronomer)
zoologist: studies animals
psychologist: studies the mind
ophthalmologist: studies the eye
gerontologist: studies aging
pathologist: studies diseases

Exercise A5
spherical – round, ball-like
zoological – about animals
astrological – about the stars
biological – about life
psychological – mental
atmospheric – about air
phonological – about sound
pathological – diseased, sick

Exercise B
1. arthritis
2. dermatitis
3. laryngitis
4. hepatitis
5. gastritis

Exercise D
Pandemic • hemispheres • disastrous
catastrophic • scenarios • typhoid
bubonic • cholera • zoonoses • endemic
cycle • diagnosed • epidemic
Pathologists • epidemiologists • biologists
genetic • pharmaceutical

Glossary of Bases

Base	Meaning	Examples
anthro	human being	anthropology, misanthrope
arch	rule, lead	anarchy, monarch, monarchy
astro	star	astronomy, astronaut
atmos	air	atmosphere
bio	life	biology, biography
cap	chief, head	capital, decapitate
capt, cept, cep, cip, ceive	get, take	captor, captive, accept, intercept, reception, recipient, receive, conceive
cede, ceed, cess	go, move	precede, intercede, proceed, exceed succeed, process
cide, cis	cut	decide, coincide, decision
claim, clam	talk, shout	acclamation, acclaim, proclaim
clud, clus	close, shut	include, conclude, seclusion
cord	agree	accord; discord
creas	grow	increase, decrease, crescent
cred	believe, trust in	credence, incredible, creditor
cur	run	currently, occur
cycle	circle	bicycle, cyclone
dem	people	democrat, epidemic
derm	skin	dermatitis, epidermis
dict	say	predict, dictate, indicate, dictionary
duce, duct	lead	produce, reduce, introduce, production, conduct, abduct
dol	sorrow	condolence
fact, fect	make, do	factory, faction, defector, perfect
fer	carry, bear	transfer, interfere, conference
fin	end, complete	final, indefinite
firm	make solid	affirmative, confirm
flat	blow	inflate, deflate, inflation
flect, flex	bend	reflect, deflect, flexible

Base	Meaning	Examples
fug	run, move	refugee, refuge, fugitive
fus	pour	confuse, diffuse, refuse
grad, gress	go, step	gradual, graduate, progress
gen	origin	genesis, genetic
geo	earth	geography, geothermal
gnos	know	diagnose, agnostic
hemi	half	hemisphere
ject	throw	project, reject, inject, subject
jud, jur	judge	judicial, jury
lect	choose	select, elect, collect
leg	law	illegal, legislature
lide, lis	strike, move	collide, collision
lit	read	illiterate, literacy
logo	word	logic, logo, dialogue
logy	study	ecology, psychology
med	middle	intermediary, immediately, media
migra	move	migratory, immigration
minis	help, serve	minister, administration
miss, mit	send	mission, commission, dismiss, permit, transmit, submit
mob, mot	move	mobile, automotive
nat	birth, nature	nation, nature, naturalize
nym	name	anonymous, antonym, synonym
ord	order	ordinary, orderly, insubordination
pathy	feeling	sympathy, antipathy, apathy
pel	push	compel, dispel, expel
pend	hang, wait	independent, suspend
pharm	drug	pharmacy, pharmaceutical
phobia	fear	claustrophobia. agoraphobia, homophobe
phon	sound	phonology, telephone
phil	love	philosophy, Anglophile
phys	nature	physics, physical
plaud, plod	clap, noise	applaud, explode
plex, plic	fold	complex, complicate

Base	Meaning	Examples
pon, pos	place, put	proponent, postpone, composer, propose, depose
port	carry	export, import, support, report, transportation
press	push	suppress, express
psych	mind	psychology, psychotic
quest	look for, ask	question, request
rect, regul	rule, manage	director, regulatory, unregulated
rupt	break	erupt, disrupt, interrupt, corruption
scrib, scrip	write	scripture, describe
secut, sequ	follow	consecutive, prosecutor, consequently
serv	save	conservative, preserve, observation
side	live, sit	resident, president, subside
soph	wisdom	sophomore, philosophy
spec, spect	see, watch	suspect, inspect, expect, prospect, speculate
spir	breathe	conspiracy, respiratory
spon	answer, promise	response, irresponsible
stat, sist, stit	stand	status, state, assistant, insist, institute
struct	build	constructive, destruction, restructure, instruct
sum	take (up)	assume, resume, consume
tain, tin	hold, keep	contain, attain, detain, continue
tens	stretch, tighten	intensive, extensive
terr	earth	territory, terrestrial, terrain
tort	twist, bend	torture, distort, tortuous
tract	pull	tractor, contract, detractor, attractive, protracted
var	change	variety, variant, invariaby
vent	come	venture, prevent, conventional
vers, vert	turn, change	diverse, subversive, divert
vestig	follow, track	investigate, investigation, vestige
vic, vinc	win, defeat	convict, convince, victorious
vid, vis	see	provide, advise, vision, supervise
viv	live	survivor, revive
voc, vok	call	vocal, revoke, invoke
volv	turn	involve, revolve
zoo	animal	zoology, zoo

WPLA Radio News Scripts

Lesson 1. Terrorist Conspiracy Uncovered

This is the WPLA News at Noon.

Cindy: This is Cindy Speakwell with the News at Noon. First, a breaking story from Statesboro. Agents from the Federal Police Agency have apparently prevented a major terrorist attack. Mike Moran, the agency's spokesperson, has announced that the suspected terrorists have been detained, and weaponry hidden in a house on West 164th Street has been confiscated. The FPA has also carried out a raid on a Westside warehouse and discovered a large amount of explosives.

Moran also reported that a wider search for additional suspects is underway and an ongoing investigation is looking into possible links with a foreign terrorist organization. Although the Statesboro cell may not be the biggest one in the Unified States, it may turn out to be the most important, said Moran.

For additional details, here is Jerry Michaels on the scene. Jerry, what else have you learned about this raid?

Jerry: Well, Cindy, The FPA is being pretty quiet about who this group is and what they are planning. We are expecting more information later in the day. We do know that five of them were seen being led out of the building under heavy guard. Apparently the suspects were renting the house from a well-known citizen of Statesboro. More on this later.

Cindy: Thanks, Jerry. We'll be following this story throughout the day.

(Lesson on page 3)

Lesson 2. Airliner, Military Aircraft Collide

WPLA Newsbreak.

Cindy: We interrupt our regularly scheduled program with a breaking news story. Flight forty-three from Gulfside Airport has apparently crashed in the Pacific Gulf. The last message from the pilot indicated that they were encountering a heavy thunderstorm, and he was attempting to fly around it.

The pilot of the twin-engine jetliner was last heard from a half-hour after takeoff on its hour-long flight to Pelagia. Air-sea rescue teams have been sent to the crash site, estimated to be about 150 air-miles offshore. A report from the searchers indicates they are experiencing a heavy rainstorm, making the search difficult.

An airline spokeswoman has confirmed that the plane was carrying a crew of five and 85 passengers. We will be following this story with updates as they become available. This is Cindy Speakwell with WPLA News. Now back to the Harry Queen talk show.

 (Lesson on page 5)

Lesson 3. Wilderness Saved

The WPLA Evening News with Walter Conrad.

Walter: Good evening, ladies and gentlemen, this is Walter Conrad with the evening news from the WPLA Newsroom in New Urban City. We are following several stories this evening, including the latest on the tragic crash of NATIONAIR's Flight 43 after takeoff from Gulfside, and we have an update on the terrorists detained on Friday in Statesboro.

We begin tonight's news with an announcement from the capitol that the National Congress has voted to close the Boreal Wilderness to further oil exploration. Forrest Woods, President of the Nature Society, has described the saving of the wilderness as a great success. The society has been conducting an intensive campaign to save the incredible beauty of the wilderness and the many plant and animal species unique to the Boreas.

The Society has been fighting the proposed plan to extract and transport oil from the wilderness for the past seven years. The reaction from environmentalists around the country has been enthusiastic. Fred Sparrow, president of the Audubon Club, has predicted that The Nature Society will receive the Presidential Good Citizen Award for its efforts. We'll be right back after this message.

(Lesson on page 8)

Lesson 4. Negotiator meets with Kidnappers

The WPLA Evening News with Walter Conrad.

Maria: Good evening. This is Maria Ventura sitting in for Walter Conrad, who is on assignment. For our top story this evening we have Jerry Michaels our roving reporter on the scene in Atlantia. We will also be bringing you updates on the ongoing terrorism investigation in Statesboro, and a report from Karl Svensky in Port Nord, where the closure of the Boreal wilderness is sending shock waves throughout the oil industry there.

But first, our top story from Jerry Michaels. Jerry, what's the latest on the kidnapping of the Antarctican ambassador?

Jerry: Well, Maria, I have just come from a press conference where the government negotiator has released a statement from the kidnappers of the ambassador. They are demanding the release of all political prisoners. We have also learned that the ambassador's political advisor and his interpreter are in the hands of the kidnappers, who have identified themselves as the AMSAT faction. The leader of the faction has issued a statement on video warning all foreign visitors and workers that they too are in danger.

At this time there is also a small demonstration at City Hall. The demonstrators are demanding a meeting with the governor. That's all we know at this time, Maria.

Maria: Thanks, Jerry, we'll be following your story closely.

(Lesson on page 13)

Lesson 5. Awards for Artists and Scientists

From New Urban City, this is the Morning Show with Maria Ventura.

Maria: Good morning from New Urban City. This is Maria Ventura. Yesterday in Norberg, the Academy of Arts and Sciences announced its annual prizes. Panelist Dr. Arthur Andrews named three scientists, a novelist, a musician, and an economist. And for the first time an award goes to an environmental activist.

Earlier this morning we talked with Dr. Andrews, a resident of Genera, who was speaking with us from his library. Here's an excerpt from our interview:

Dr. Andrews, this year the Academy gave an award to an environmentalist. This is a first, isn't it?

Andrews: Oh, yes. It is very clear that although chemists, botanists, geologists, and other scientists do very valuable work, the time has come to recognize the importance of the work of environmentalists such as the Arcadian forestry expert Robert Rackham and the ecologist Nkwe Ngwa, who has done so much research on the Saharan Desert.

Maria: This year for the first time, an Antillian dissident won the award for his literary contributions. But as a dissident, he is not welcome in Antillia. Is the Academy making a political statement?

Andrews: The Academy is always making a statement, whether the award goes to an Antillian or a Ruritanian or a Slobovian or a Zanzanian. Our statement is simple: we recognize and award contributions to world peace.

Maria: Thank you so much for speaking to us, Dr. Andrews.

Andrews: You're quite welcome.

Maria: And now this:

(Lesson on page 17)

Lesson 6. Nonresident Policy Questioned

The WPLA Evening News with Walter Conrad.

Walter: Good evening. Tonight we are going to have an interview with the Antillian novelist Pedro Garcia, and later we'll hear from economist Martin Greenberg. But first we go to Lowland, where Jerry Michaels is standing by with the latest on the nonresident policy debate. Jerry, what's going on there in Kapitalia?

Jerry: Walter, I spoke earlier with Independent Senator C. N. Unsap, who is highly critical of the government's inability or unwillingness to take action on the illegal immigration issue. Unsap is also unhappy with the government's willingness to accept over two million refugees last year. He claims that the influx of uneducated entrants is a major cause of unemployment among Lowland's own native population, and that the recent labor unrest in the city of Portonovo is a result of admitting so many unskilled workers. Unsap has called the government's response irresponsible and unproductive.

Walter: Jerry, has the government's own United Democracy Front issued a defense?

Jerry: Yes, Walter. At a press conference today, Senator Libby of the UDF defended the refugee program by pointing out that many refugees were taking jobs that Lowlanders find unattractive. Libby called Unsap's position a lot of nonsense, saying that noncitizens are making an unquestionable contribution to Lowland society.

Walter: Thank you, Jerry, for shedding some light on a very unclear issue there in Lowland.

 (Lesson on page 21)

Lesson 7. Candidates Disagree

This is the WPLA News at Noon.

Cindy: This is Cindy Speakwell with the News at Noon. With me is Walter Conrad, who was there last night at the debate between I. M. Contra and Dr. Changeless. Walter, who won?

Walter: Well, Cindy, it would be a mistake to say there was a winner. Contra probably scored points with the environmentalists by claiming that the administration is apathetic in its so-called support of antipollution policies. And of course, Changeless had difficulty dismissing Contra's criticism of the administration's handling of the Karl Robb affair. Contra called the misappropriation of millions of dollars a malignancy that has poisoned the government like a cancer.

Cindy: And how did Changeless respond?

Walter: Angrily, of course, and as usual Changeless wasted no words. She attacked the Everyman Party calling them misfits and malcontents who were misguided, maladjusted, amoral atheists. She went on to say that the EP's tactics had misfired.

Cindy: Thank you, Walter. The public reaction to the debate is still coming in, and we will see whose tactics have misfired. Watch the polls. We'll take a break, and when we come back we'll talk with Serena Placid on what's going on with the anti-war movement.

(Lesson on page 23)

Lesson 8. Pan-Equatorian Organization Meets

From New Urban City, this is the Morning Show with Maria Ventura.

Maria: Good morning from New Urban City. This is Maria Ventura welcoming you to the Morning Show. Later in the program we'll be hearing from I.M. Contra and her latest disagreements with Dr. Changeless, and we'll be interviewing Senator Libby on the government's nonresident policy. But first, with us from Tropica is Dr. E. E. Sango reporting on the Pan-Equatorian conference in Tropica. Dr. Sango, did the tri-state area accomplish anything at the conference?

Sango: Hello, Maria, and yes, I think we did. First, we are going forward on a multimillion dollar hydroelectric plant. And our three capitals will now be connected by a high speed monorail. And we're also looking into a shared solar power project that will help unify our three small nations.

Maria: It seems that developing infrastructure was the theme of the conference.

Sango: Education was also on our agenda. You know we currently have a regional polytechnic institute, and we are developing plans for a new bilingual university in Occidentia. All students will graduate with fluency in French and English, and actually most will be trilingual since they have a native language.

Maria: That sounds promising. What other projects might be developed?

Sango: At our next semiannual meeting in Savanna we hope to develop uniform trade and immigration policies among our three nations.

Maria: It looks like we are running out of time, Dr. Sango, so thank you so much for your time. We'll be back after this:

(Lesson on page 26)

Lesson 9. Courtroom Drama Intensifies

This is the WPLA News at Noon.

Cindy: This is Cindy Speakwell with the News at Noon. We have just learned that the beloved ex-president of Territoria and statesman R. J. Lee has died. There are no further details at this time. Walter Conrad will have more on the evening news. Our lead story this afternoon is the ongoing trial of alleged drug king Juan Solo. Standing by at the courthouse in San Tomaso is Jerry Michaels to enlighten us on the latest developments. Jerry, what's the latest?

Jerry: Cindy, the prosecution has brought in a new witness, Julio Doble. When Solo recognized Doble he seemed to realize immediately that he was in trouble. On the witness stand, Doble identified Solo and claimed Solo had employed him to be the leader of a gang of thugs who terrorized northeastern Andea. Doble also implicated Solo in the assassination of a rival drug lord Carlos "el tigre" Ramos.

Cindy: So what was Solo's reaction?

Jerry: He was bewildered and visibly weakened by Dobles's testimony. The prosecutors immediately capitalized on Solo's befuddled state. Doble's accusations enabled the prosecution to extract important information from Solo.

Cindy: Will this lead to widening and deepening the investigation of the influence of the drug empire?

Jerry: That's what it looks like. The arrest this afternoon of Pablo Portillo probably indicates that the government is ready to strengthen and intensify their campaign in Andea.

Cindy: Thanks, Jerry. And now this:

(Lesson on page 30)

Lesson 10. Leader of Independence Movement Dies

The WPLA Evening News with Walter Conrad.

Walter: Good evening, ladies and gentlemen, this is Walter Conrad with the evening news from the WPLA newsroom in New Urban City.

Tonight's lead story is about the passing of a truly great leader, R. J. Lee, former president of Territoria. A modern-day Abraham Lincoln, Lee came from a poor neighborhood in the provincial city of Interioria. Lee always credited his successful leadership of the Unity party and his country to lessons learned from his grandfather, a man who also dreamed of independence and equality for his homeland.

Through experiences as a mine worker, he learned the value and power of peaceful, well-organized protests and strikes. He was particularly noted for his tolerance, fairness, and commitment to equality. His passion to bring independence to Territoria led him into politics and the eventual founding of the Unity Party, well known for its policy of civil disobedience. From Territoria, we have this comment from the current president, Jason Burkhart:

Burkhart: Lee was always about fairness and opportunity, and he was determined to lead the nation toward independence. And then after we gained independence, he continued to work both nationally and internationally for the betterment of mankind. His election to the presidency in 1962 enabled him to extend his influence and adherence to nonviolence to other countries and thus brought him recognition as a great statesman.

Walter: Territoria, and indeed the world, has lost a beloved citizen and public servant. But his contributions will long be remembered. He died as he lived, peacefully. Stay with us; there's more to come.

(Lesson on page 33)

Lesson 11. Assassination Investigation

Maria: If you've just tuned in, this is the Morning Show and I'm Maria Ventura. We're talking about the assassination Tuesday of King Hamad III.

Just two days ago terrorism robbed the tiny peaceful kingdom of Burania of its monarch, King Hamad III. The king was riding in an open carriage on his way to a palace reception when a bomb thrown into the carriage exploded and killed him.

Although the king's bodyguards shot and killed the assassin moments after the attack, the government has not revealed any information concerning the identification of the assassin.

We go now to Jerry Michaels in Burania. Jerry, how are the people reacting?

Jerry: Well, Maria, people are going back to work and shops are opening up, so things are getting back to normal. Prince Mahad spoke this morning to citizens of the kingdom, and I quote:

"Fellow citizens, thank you for your expressions of sympathy for me, my family, and the nation. I call on you not to allow terrorism to gain the upper hand. Anarchy seeks disruption but we must work for the continuation of my father, the king's, peaceful and progressive rule. We must remain calm."

Also Maria, we have learned that shortly after the explosion, the palace received a communication from an alleged member of an outlawed group, the Organization for Democratic Nationalism. The caller praised the dead assassin, saying, "He has attained martyrdom and others will follow in his footsteps."

Maria: Thanks for the update, Jerry. In spite of the tragedy, it sounds as if there is stability and order in Burania. And now on to other news.

(Lesson on page 37)

Lesson 12. First Annual World Series

This is the WPLA News at Noon.

Cindy: Hello. I'm Cindy Speakwell, and this is the news at noon.

First, a quick update on the memorial services for R. J. Lee. Countless people lined the streets as the golden funeral carriage moved slowly along Independence Avenue toward Lee's final resting place at the National Cemetery. And in Burania, the official report from Major General Adam seems to indicate that the actual cause of King Hamad's death was a gunshot wound. And now on to our top story; we go to Jerry Michaels in Japan.

Jerry: Thanks, Cindy. The first annual world series of baseball is over, and the sporting world is stunned as a result of the incredible victory of the Hiroshima Carp over the Washington Nationals.

Cindy: And how are the Nationals taking it?

Jerry: Well, Cindy, with considerable disappointment, as you might expect. The Nationals played flawless baseball through six playoff games, and perhaps they became too comfortable with their easy success. In the final game Manager Billy Green called on dependable Lefty Jackson to pitch with only three days' rest – a reasonable and logical decision because Jackson has been unbeatable this year. And Jackson's performance was indeed special – he was tireless until the final inning, when with two outs, Hiroshima put together an incredible rally. With the bases full, and a golden opportunity for Kaz Matsui, Green called on his reliable closer Bill Robinson. One pitch – one swing. And Hiroshima walked off with the golden trophy. That wraps up the game and the season, Cindy.

Cindy: Thanks, Jerry. We'll be right back with new information about the earthquake in Kosharam.

(Lesson on page 41)

Lesson 13. Disastrous Earthquake in Kosharam

The WPLA Evening News with Walter Conrad.

Walter: Good evening, ladies and gentlemen. I'm Walter Conrad with the evening news from WPLA in New Urban City. Our first story takes us to the city of Kashkar in mountainous Kosharam, where a disastrous earthquake Sunday morning killed hundreds and destroyed many villages.

This region is accustomed to minor tremors but has not seen a powerful earthquake of this magnitude for many generations. Many of the ordinary houses on these rocky slopes were built prior to the establishment of the Regulatory Building Commission, and for that reason were not in compliance with the new laws requiring sturdy foundations. The quake measured 7.2 on the Richter scale. The strength of the quake plus hilly terrain and unusually rainy weather the previous week resulted in dangerous landslide conditions.

There was serious damage to some buildings in the capital, but there was no obvious damage to the capitol building itself. Although secondary shock waves struck Monday, most of the disastrous impact came from the primary quake Sunday morning.

Voluntary organizations worldwide have responded with generous donations and helpful assistance. Survivors are being housed in temporary shelters and are grateful for the immediate thoughtful responses from around the world. A parliamentary session promised financial assistance and help from the military. Later in the program we'll have a live report from Jerry Michaels, but first, this message:

(Lesson on page 44)

Lesson 14. Dramatic Rescue at Island Park

From New Urban City, this is the Morning Show with Maria Ventura.

Maria: Good morning from New Urban City and welcome to the Morning Show. Yesterday Placidboro in Wabbassetshire was the scene of a dramatic rescue. As happens every spring, the frozen river thawed and broke up into blocks of ice. Sometimes massive blocks of ice flowing in the swollen river can pile up along the banks or ram into structures that are too close to the river. One such structure, historic Island Park Casino, on an island in the river, was destroyed. Fortunately the casino is inactive during the winter months, but Eli Sharp, caretaker of the casino, was trapped on the island. Despite a heroic effort, rescuers were unable to reach the island due to the current and destructive nature of the ice blocks. Fortunately Sharp was rescued by a police helicopter.

We have Frank Chance, owner of Island Park Casino, on the line here. Mr. Chance, How is Mr. Sharp, and what happened to the building?

Chance: Well, Eli was a little feverish, but he was basically OK. The building—ah, geez, it was a classic, you know. Built in 1874—a thing of beauty and a center of activity for all ages. But the ice and water took it down in 20 minutes! It just tumbled down and then floated off in pieces.

Maria: I'm sure it was tragic to see such extensive damage to your livelihood. Will you rebuild?

Chance: I'll have to think about that first. For now, I'm just thankful that Eli Sharp is safe, and we're all grateful for the unselfish actions of the rescuers. They were terrific, and thanks to the decisive action of Police Chief Standish, the helicopter arrived just in time.

Maria: Thank you for speaking with us during this difficult time, Mr. Chance.

Chance: Thank you, Maria.

Maria: And now a check on the weather with Samantha Summers:

(Lesson on page 47)

Lesson 15. Climate Change Definitely Here?

The WPLA Evening News with Walter Conrad.

Walter: Good evening, ladies and gentlemen. I'm Walter Conrad with the evening news from WPLA in New Urban City. At the top of the hour we turn to Jerry Michaels in Nova Arkansk to report on the conclusion of an important summit conference on the state of the environment. Jerry, how has this conference been different from so many others?

Jerry: Well, that's a good question, Walter. This isn't the first time we've reported that an internationally known group of scientists has issued dramatically worded statements on the greenhouse effect. As before, environmentalists have warned that we will see steadily rising temperatures, a rise in ocean levels, and coastal flooding. In fact, this conference concluded with some scientists saying it is probably too late. That's what is different.

Walter: Are there particular areas that will be affected more significantly than others?

Jerry: The developing nations will definitely be hit harder. We expect to see significantly altered agricultural conditions globally. Islands and coastal areas will be inundated, and if you consider that one third of the world's population lives in mainland coastal areas, it's clear that this can significantly and severely affect the world.

This of course will result in negative effects, politically and economically, especially in Asia and the Pacific region. The report concluded by emphasizing that a multinational effort of all nations must be undertaken immediately; otherwise civilization will slip backward.

Walter: Thank you, Jerry. We'll be back momentarily with an update on relief efforts in Kosharam.

Lesson 16. FTBU Protests Intracoastal Beach Conference

This is the WPLA News at Noon.

Cindy: This is Cindy Speakwell with the News at Noon. We're following several stories today. We have a preview of the agenda for the ICPC's intercontinental conference on population control, and as we reported yesterday, protesters are planning to prevent the pre-conference workshop at Pelagia. Jerry Michaels is in Pelagia, and this morning he interviewed Doctor J. P. Ahmedi.

Jerry, what's Ahmedi's response to the threat of interference from the FTBU group?

Jerry: Cindy, Dr. Ahmedi has insisted that the Intracoastal Conference will not be interrupted or postponed.

Cindy: And what do we hear from the FTBU?

Jerry: Well, W. W. Stoppit's advisor and interpreter reiterated Stoppit's basic positions on contraceptives, extramarital sex, and abortion. As you know, Cindy, thousands of protesters have been here in Pelagia all week planning to disrupt the pre-conference workshop. In a post-demonstration announcement, the leader of the demonstrators introduced Stoppit to the crowd.

Cindy: And what was the reaction?

Jerry: Extraordinary, Cindy. Stoppit threw away his prepared remarks and predicted that the FTBU would have thousands of demonstrators at the ICPC conference next week. He said that the demonstration would be unprecedented.

Cindy: So, Jerry, it looks like today's protest was just a simple prelude to next week's conflict in Intracoastal Beach. And now on to other news.

Lesson 17. Subcommittee Reports on Subversive Activity

The WPLA Evening News with Walter Conrad.

Walter: Good evening, ladies and gentlemen, this is Walter Conrad with the evening news from the WPLA Newsroom in New Urban City. We'll be following up on the ICPC Intracoastal Beach conference, and we'll hear from Jerry Michaels, who is at the epicenter of the earthquake in Kosharam. But first from Holm, Nordia, the subcommittee on un-Nordic activity has released its annual report on subversive activities.

The annual review included new details on the attempted assassination of Detective Supervisor Gridlock Homes. Homes survived the attack in a suburban subway by disabling the attacker with pepper spray and wrestling the submachine gun out of the attacker's hands.

We have also learned that superspy Doctor Oui has been apprehended, on a subtropical island. The details of the episode revealed that Oui's capture occurred just hours before he planned to board his hyperspeed submarine. Agent James Stock had parachuted onto the island and with two other agents subdued Oui in his office, using a hypodermic injection to tranquilize Oui, who was then transported to a Nordian surface ship.

And finally, the Interior Ministry is considering the establishment of a Superbureau of Investigation. All surveillance of suspected subversive activity would be centralized in the new agency. And now this message:

(Lesson on page 59)

Lesson 18. Exports Exceed Imports

From New Urban City, this is the Morning Show with Maria Ventura.

Maria: Good morning from New Urban City. This is Maria Ventura welcoming you to the Morning Show. Later this morning we'll be talking with superhero James Stock and expect to hear more about his exciting episode in Epicuria. We'll begin our first hour this morning with the market report with James Moneyminder.

Moneyminder: Thanks, Maria. The trading on Fed Street was intensive yesterday. The stock market exceeded expectations thanks to a last minute surge based on significant advances in earnings from the transportation industry. The Johnson-Dow index was also up. Apparently, losses from the declining housing market were absorbed by expansion of the solar energy industry.

Maria: Thank you, James. And now we have heard that several inside sources are projecting a continued upward trend. They believe the business community sees the global economy as alive and well, and that economic progress in several areas is here to stay. One positive indication comes to us from Newlandia, where Jane Doe filed this report.

Doe: This is Jane Doe reporting from Newlandia, where the Ministry of Finance and Trade announced that exports exceeded imports for the first quarter of the year. Increased production of textiles and electronics has contributed to this minor explosion of the overall economy. The administration has admitted that the maritime transportation project has fallen below production goals, but plans are underway to expand this important industry. Jane Doe, reporting for the Morning Show.

(Lesson on page 63)

Lesson 19. Students Demand Chancellor's Resignation

This is the WPLA News at Noon.

Cindy: This is Cindy Speakwell with the News at Noon. In Xenostan, Students for Free Expression are engaged in a major demonstration outside the administration building of National University. Chanting "Rehire or retire," the demonstrators are aiming their anger at the chancellor because of his recent decision to revise the curriculum and reduce the faculty. The chancellor's actions are based on the government's program to de-emphasize dependence on the West. As a result, the university has replaced all expatriate English instructors and reduced the courses and programs taught by other Westerners.

In a recent speech, the president of Xenostan declared that the West was a degenerate society, and that the influence of foreign workers and visitors could destabilize the Xenostanian Revolution and destroy the unique culture of Xenostan.

Last week the SFE secretly selected a committee to meet with the administration, and today the committee released its demands to rehire faculty, reinstate important programs, and fire the chancellor. We'll be watching this developing story.

And the latest from the Transcontinental Airline strike is that the union has rejected ownership's latest offer. Ownership has defended their position, saying that decreases in profits have forced this decision. Later today we'll hear more about this from Jerry Michaels. And that's all for now.

(Lesson on page 67)

Lesson 20. Union Sympathizers Walk off the Job

The WPLA Evening News with Walter Conrad.

Walter: Good evening, ladies and gentlemen, this is Walter Conrad with the evening news from the WPLA Newsroom in New Urban City. We'll be reporting on the latest from Xenostan, where, according to our contacts there, demonstrations are continuing as the students are objecting to the government's Xenostan First policy. We'll also be looking ahead to the conclusion of the meeting of world health officials in Genera. But our top story this evening is the Transcontinental Airways strike at airports throughout the Northeast. Air travel is in turmoil as pilots and flight attendants refuse to cross picket lines in sympathy with the Ground Crew Union. So far, negotiators have failed to reach a compromise, talks have collapsed, and there is no contract. The union has objected to the 10% increase offered by the airline. Meriwether P. Barnstormer, principal owner of TCA, insists he is ready to cooperate, but competition is forcing him to continue the conditions of the present contract for one more year. He continues to be opposed to anything more than 10 percent.

And now we turn to Cindy Speakwell, who recently interviewed Barnstormer and the president of the Ground Crew Union.

Cindy: Walter, union leaders have insisted that TCA is making contradictory offers to them. According to William Walker, president of the union, Barnstormer says one thing, and the negotiator says another. Walker went on to say, "We make a counter-offer, the negotiator seems to be sympathetic, and then Barnstormer continues to be contrary and contradictory. This can't continue," concluded the union president. So there you have it, Walter. It looks like a stalemate for now.

Walter: Thanks, Cindy. And now this message:

(Lesson on page 71)

Lesson 21. World Health Officials Warn: Pandemic Inevitable

From New Urban City, this is the Morning Show with Maria Ventura.

Maria: Good morning from New Urban City. This is Maria Ventura welcoming you to the Morning Show. With us today in the studio is Jerry Michaels, just back from a major conference of world health officials. Jerry, we understand that these officials representing organizations in both hemispheres have declared that a pandemic is imminent. Can you clarify that for us?

Jerry: Certainly, Maria. There have been many pandemics in human history, and it seems that with our shrinking world, epidemics can become pandemic very quickly.

Maria: Jerry, what is the difference between epidemic and pandemic?

Jerry: Maria, as you know, "pan" means, essentially, "all," whereas "epi" indicates a center. In other words an epidemic is somewhat restricted to one area, but a pandemic is worldwide.

Maria: I see, and just who are these world health officials?

Jerry: Well, they're biologists, pathologists, epidemiologists, and even zoologists.

Maria: Why are zoologists involved?

Jerry: Because a pandemic may actually be a disease transmitted from animals to humans, like the Asian Bird Flu we're hearing about.

Maria: Should we be worried, Jerry?

Jerry: Absolutely, Maria. A pandemic can be disastrous, affecting every aspect of human life, even our biosphere, all life forms on planet Earth.

Maria: Is there any good news, Jerry?

Jerry: Yes, certainly. Our scientists say we have the ability to develop a sophisticated international pandemic plan, and at this time there is no need to panic.

Maria: Thank you, Jerry. That's all for the Morning Show. Stay tuned to WPLA. We'll hear from Daniel Goodwell with his weekly commentary on the News at Noon.

(Lesson on page 75)

Lesson 22. Poverty, Terror, and Climate Change

Cindy: And so this is Cindy Speakwell wrapping up the noontime news. Finally, today's commentary by Daniel Goodwell:

Daniel: At last, as I have been saying for months, even years, there is a growing realization that terrorism is not just about religion or nationalism or some fanatic belief. Today, the UN officially recognized the connection between climate change, degradation of the environment, and terrorism.

Certainly, terrorist acts are and have been committed in the name of some belief or out of hatred for a specific government or group of people, but an increasingly dangerous cause of terrorism is something all of us are to blame for. We treat Mother Nature badly. And in fact I have often said that one day Mother Nature will punish us in ways that far exceed the damage from bombs and bullets. We are changing our precious and fragile environment. The biosphere that we know today is under assault from reckless development, over-consumption, overpopulation, insufficient government control, and just plain carelessness and laziness. Buy it, use it, throw it away. Anywhere. Anything. And in the process of making and using, we are putting incredible strains on our atmosphere, our protective shield that allows our life forms to exist. The climate changes. The earth and its atmosphere warm up. Sea levels rise. Deserts expand. Millions are displaced. Anger, resentment, crime, and yes, terrorism run rampant.

The time has come for concerted international action! I welcome the UN's leadership, and I challenge my own country to do the same. This is Daniel Goodwell, thanking you for listening and urging you to act.

(Lesson on page 79)

Key Words from the Radio News Scripts

Note: Words repeated in the broadcast are given only once in the following lists.

Lesson 1: *Terrorist Conspiracy Uncovered*
Inflections

news*	detained	links	expecting
breaking	hidden	biggest	later
Agents	confiscated	Unified	seen
prevented	carried	States	renting
agency's	discovered	most**	More**
has	explosives	said	Thanks
announced	reported	details	following
suspected	wider	learned	
terrorists	suspects	being	
been	looking	planning	

* *news* has no singular form.
 ** *most* and *more* are irregular adjectival forms like *better* and *best*.

Radio script on page 91

Lesson 2: *Airliner, Military Aircraft Collide*
Compounds

Newsbreak	twin-engine	Air-sea	spokeswoman
forty-three	jetliner	air-miles	updates
Gulfside	half-hour	offshore	talk show
Airport	takeoff	rainstorm	
thunderstorm	hour-long	airline	

Radio script on page 92

Lesson 3: *Wilderness Saved*
Common Bases

detained	intensive	extract	predicted
described	incredible	transport	receive
conducting	proposed	reaction	

Radio script on page 93

Lesson 4: *Negotiator Meets with Kidnappers*
-er Noun Suffix

reporter	kidnappers	interpreter	workers
ambassador	prisoners	leader	demonstrators
negotiator	advisor	visitors	governor

Radio script on page 94

Lesson 5: *Awards for Artists and Scientists*
Other "Doer" Suffixes and "Place" Suffixes

Panelist	resident	forestry	literary
scientists	library	ecologist	Ruritanian
novelist	chemists	Antillian	Slobovian
musician	botanists	dissident	Zanzanian
economist	geologists		
activist	environmentalists		

Radio script on page 95

Lesson 6: *Nonresident Policy Questioned*
Negative Prefixes: *un-, in-, non-*

inability	uneducated	irresponsible	noncitizens
unwillingness	unemployment	unproductive	unquestionable
illegal	unrest	unattractive	unclear
unhappy	unskilled	nonsense	

Radio script on page 96

Lesson 7: *Candidates Disagree*
Negative Prefixes: *anti-, a-, dis-, mal-, mis-*

mistake	malignancy	misguided	atheists
apathetic	misfits	maladjusted	misfired
antipollution	malcontents	amoral	antiwar
dismissing			
misappropriation			

Radio script on page 97

Lesson 8: *Pan-Equatorian Organization Meets*
Quantity Prefixes: *uni-, mono-, bi-, tri-, pan-, multi-, semi-, poly-, equi-*

Pan-Equatorian	monorail	bilingual	semiannual
tri-state	unify	trilingual	uniform
multimillion	polytechnic		

Radio script on page 98

Lesson 9: *Courtroom Drama Intensifies*
Verb Prefixes and Suffixes: *en-, -en, be-, -ify, -ize, -ate*

enlighten	terrorized	capitalized	deepening
realize	implicated	befuddled	indicates
identified	bewildered	enabled	strengthen
employed	weakened	widening	intensify

Radio script on page 99

Lesson 10: *Leader of Independence Movement Dies*
Noun Suffixes: *-ance/-ence, -ity, -hood, -ship, -ness*

president	independence	fairness	influence
neighborhood	equality	disobedience	adherence
leadership	experiences	opportunity	nonviolence
Unity	tolerance	presidency	

Radio script on page 100

Lesson 11: *Assassination Investigation*
Noun Suffixes: *-ion, -ment, -ism, -age, -dom*

assassination	reception	expressions	communication
terrorism	government	disruption	Organization
kingdom	information	continuation	Nationalism
carriage	identification	explosion	martyrdom

Radio script on page 101

Lesson 12: *First Annual World Series*
Adjective Suffixes *-able, -less, -al, -en*

memorial	National	considerable	logical
Countless	official	flawless	unbeatable
golden	actual	comfortable	tireless
funeral	annual	dependable	reliable
final	incredible	reasonable	

Radio script on page 102

Lesson 13: *Disastrous Earthquake in Kosharam*
Adjective Suffixes *-ful, -y, -ous, -ary*

mountainous	sturdy	secondary	grateful
disastrous	hilly	primary	thoughtful
powerful	rainy	Voluntary	parliamentary
ordinary	dangerous	generous	financial
rocky	serious	helpful	military (noun)
Regulatory	obvious	temporary	

Radio script on page 103

Lesson 14: *Dramatic Rescue at Island Park*
Adjective Suffixes: *-ish, -ic, -ive*

dramatic	heroic	activity	terrific
massive	destructive	tragic	decisive
historic	feverish	extensive	
inactive	classic	unselfish	

Radio script on page 104

Lesson 15: *Climate Change Definitely Here?*
Adverb Suffixes: *-ly, -ward, -wise*

internationally	significantly	politically	otherwise
dramatically	definitely	economically	backward
steadily	globally	especially	momentarily
probably	severely	immediately	

Radio script on page 105

Lesson 16: *FTBU Protests Intracoastal Beach Conference*
Position Prefixes: *pre-, post-, inter-, intro-/intra-, extro-/extra-, contra-, ante-*

preview	interviewed	interpreter	introduced
intercontinental	interference	contraceptives	Extraordinary
protesters	Intracoastal	extramarital	prepared
prevent	interrupted	post-	predicted
pre-conference	postponed	demonstration	unprecedented
			prelude

Radio script on page 106

Lesson 17: *Subcommittee Reports on Subversive Activity*
Relationship Prefixes: *super-, sur-, sub-, para-, epi-, hyper-, hypo-*

epicenter	subway	hyperspeed	surface
subcommittee	submachine	submarine	Superbureau
subversive	superspy	parachuted	surveillance
Supervisor	subtropical	subdued	suspected
suburban	episode	hypodermic	

Radio script on page 107

Lesson 18: *Exports Exceed Imports*
Movement Prefixes: *ex-, in-/im-, ad-, ab-, trans-, pro-*

exciting	industry	progress	administration
intensive	index	indication	admitted
exceeded	absorbed	exports	project
expectations	expansion	imports	production
advances	inside	Increased	expand
transportation	projecting	explosion	important

Radio script on page 108

Lesson 19: *Students Demand Chancellor's Resignation*
Movement Prefixes: *de-, re-, se-*

demonstration (de-= completely)		destabilize	developing
administration	de-emphasize	destroy	rejected
rehire	dependence	secretly	defended
retire	result	selected	decreases
decision	replaced	released	
revise	declared	demands	
reduce	degenerate	reinstate	

Radio script on page 109

Lesson 20: *Union Sympathizers Walk off the Job*
"With" and "Against" Prefixes: *syn-, co-, contra-*

contacts	compromise	competition	sympathetic
continuing	collapsed	conditions	contrary
conclusion	contract	contradictory	concluded
sympathy	cooperate	counter-offer	

Radio script on page 110

Lesson 21: *Pandemic Inevitable*
Greek Bases and Affixes

hemispheres	biologists	zoologists	scientists
pandemic	pathologists	disastrous	sophisticated
epidemics	epidemiologists	biosphere	

Radio script on page 111

Lesson 22: *Poverty, Terror, and Climate Change*
Review of Bases, Affixes, and Compounds

Bases

realization
nationalism
recognized
connection
degradation
environment
committed
specific
government
increasingly
exceed
biosphere
development
consumption
population
insufficient
process
incredible
atmosphere
protective
expand
displaced
resentment
concerted
international
action
leadership

Affixes

commentary
realization
terrorism
nationalism
fanatic
officially
recognized
connection
degradation
environment
terrorist
committed
specific
government
increasingly
dangerous
badly

exceed
development
consumption
population
insufficient
carelessness
laziness
process
incredible
protective
expand
displaced
resentment
concerted
international
action
leadership

Compounds

noontime
climate change
anywhere
anything
life forms
Sea levels

Radio script on page 112

Other Books of Interest from Pro Lingua

All Around America. High beginner to Advanced. The basic text includes eighteen talk shows with accompanying CD's and Workbook. The radio talk show host travels around the United States visiting important places in American history. People from the past call in to explain what happened.

Lexicarry. All Levels. A vocabulary builder that features over 2500 captionless pictures. An English word list is at the back of the book, and word lists in ten other languages are available as booklets or free on the web. The illustrations are grouped into Communicative Functions, Sequences, Related Actions, Operations, Topics, Places, and Proverbs and Sayings.

The Idiom Book: 1010 Idioms in 101 Two-Page Lessons. Intermediate to Advanced. Each lesson begins with a short conversation showcasing ten idioms. The conversations are available on two CD's. *Photocopyable.*

Write After Input: Developing Paragraphs and Compositions from Listenings and Readings. Intermediate. The students are carefully guided through a series of activities that help them develop their writing skills. The activities are based on a variety of newspaper articles (the input) that the students respond to by writing.

Dictations for Discussion. Intermediate to Advanced. A text with a variety of dictation activities. The full dictations are in the back of the book for the teacher to read. Two CD's with the dictations are also available. Most of the dictations are adapted from newspaper articles.

Interactive Dictations. Intermediate. Similar to Dictations for Discussion, this text also has a CD and uses many newspaper articles as the dictations.

This World of Ours. Advanced. Issues and Aspects of Mass Culture. The text offers four sections: Interactive problem solving for small groups, Cooperative pairwork activities, Readings and dictations on pop culture, and Having fun with language. *Photocopyable.*

In My Opinion. Intermediate to Advanced. Fifty controversial contemporary topics for speaking and listening practice. *Photocopyable.*

Verdicts. Intermediate to Advanced. A selection of real court cases (torts) to be read, discussed, and decided by the class acting as a jury. The actual decisions are given. There is never a simple right answer, which promotes lively discussion and critical thinking. *Photocopyable.*

For more information or to order,
call 800-366-4775 or visit our webstore at
www.ProLinguaAssociates.com